IN PURSUIT OF THE PROMISED LAND

MIKE HARDY

End Game Press books may be purchased in bulk at special discounts for sales promotion, corporate gifts, ministry, fund-raising, or educational purposes. Special editions can also be created to specifications. For details, contact Special Sales Dept., End Game Press, P.O. Box 206, Nesbit, MS 38651 or info@endgamepress.com.

Visit our website at www.endgamepress.com.

Library of Congress Control Number: 2024902016
HB ISBN: 9781637972137
PB ISBN: 9781637972144
eBook ISBN: 9781637972151

Cover by Dan Pitts
Interior Design by Typewriter Creative Co.

Printed in the United States of America
10 9 8 7 6 5 4 3 2 1

This book is dedicated to Len and Virginia Rogers—thank you for never giving up. I always saw Christ in you. Thank you.

I want to thank the Holy Spirit for constant intercession through the entire writing process. Thank you to my beautiful wife Judy for her daily love and patience. Her encouragement, listening ear and feedback was monumental. Thank you to Eric for calling me and encouraging me weekly. Thank you to David P. for being an inspiration. Lastly, thank you to Victoria and Michelle and all the staff at End Game. I am so glad I sat at that lunch table the first day of the conference. I have no words, this side of Heaven, to express my gratitude for your patience, guidance, and godliness—thank you for believing in me and my story.

CONTENTS

1

SHORT-TERM GAIN = LONG-TERM PAIN

Day One

Maple syrup and burgers. That's what I first remember about that March twilight in 1995—the fragrance of syrup blended with that greasy air that is emitted from a restaurant exhaust fan. Though it was only March, it was already humid in Miami. The breeze was blowing, but it wasn't much relief. I rolled up the car windows and cranked up the AC, but soon switched it back off and rolled the windows down again. Neither choice provided much comfort.

Damp with sweat, my shirt stuck to the leather car seats. But it wasn't from the hot air.

I smacked my dry lips, nerves wracking my whole body. I was convinced my shotgun passenger could hear every valve of my heart open and shut. I was not anticipating a medical diagnosis, though my heart surely needed examination.

The police and DEA were not at the top of my mental list of concerns, either, though they should have been. No, I was nervous that I would not receive the package, and "Christmas" would be spoiled. Christmas in March. And Santa was not bringing this gift.

"Please," I muttered, finally verbalizing my stress, "let this guy show up with the package."

The last three hours had allowed me to see plenty of what Miami had to offer: strip malls, fast food joints, Cuban coffee shops peddling liquid speed, street vendors selling churros, that wonderful Cuban donut. But I had seen enough. I was like a horse with its blinders securely in place. I was focused only on one thing—getting my package.

We have been sitting still, as an anchor securely on the seafloor. A darkness and eeriness seems to be encompassing the car. Of course, this is a byproduct of nervousness and uncertainty. Anyway, we are stationed in my vehicle in the parking lot of a local pancake house. My watch seemed to be working against me—every fourth or fifth glance revealed only one more minute had gone by. I had a lot riding on this transaction.

A slight opening of the windows once again brought my attention to that musty maple syrup smell. I breathed in deeply. That scent took me back to our family restaurant back in Key West. The memory stood in sweet yet stark contrast to my current situation. Back there, the scent of pancakes meant pleasure, not danger. No, our restaurant in the heart of New

Key West was a sanctuary of safety and security. My son, just thirteen-months-old, loved the mini pancakes we served there.

For a moment, I hesitated. Something in the back of my mind told me, *Get out now.*

But I shoved that thought back down as quickly as it had come. Now wasn't the time to back down. I was finally becoming a "big time" gangster.

All that time watching *The Godfather* had prepared me for this moment. The mob stories my dad had told me, the secret life he had lived, was now living out in front of me. Finally, a chance to participate with my father in an area I could please him. I felt confident I could do this kind of work well. I was determined to see this transaction through.

Just the day before, the arrangements were set in stone. The boss had told me "You're not to touch anything or be near any packages."

Who was he kidding? I was a gangster. I had it covered.

Just three hours earlier I'd handed over $40,000 in cash— what would have been a year's salary back at the restaurant— to a twenty-year-old I hardly knew. Now, I was expecting the package it had paid for: two kilos of cocaine and some anxiety relief.

My buddy and I had been waiting three hours for our delivery. The delivery location seemed to be an issue; it must have been because we had visited a dozen locations. It was a cruel irony that we eventually ended up at this pancake house, which smelled so much like the security of home—either that, or the provision of a higher power reminding me of the life I'd thrown away. But if there was a God trying to speak to me, I was not listening.

The night had dragged on far too long, and we were way over schedule. My phone rang. I picked it up.

"Where is that guy with our package?" the boss's voice rang out. This was the fifth time he'd called.

I had no answers, but I repeated what I'd been told. "Just fifteen minutes."

I'd been asking myself the same question. We might have just lost $40,000. My moment to shine was diminishing.

My mind raced, coming up with all kinds of scenarios for how this might play out. How would the package be delivered? With all the movies I'd seen, my imagination had spiraled. At that point I was imagining an event on par with the best "Miami Vice" had to offer.

The phone rang again. My partner answered. After a moment he said "Flash your lights three times."

Ten seconds later, there was a knock on the passenger window. My buddy rolled it down, and a backpack passed through, obscuring the delivery man's face from my line of sight. We were at the point of no return now. It was done, and in my mind, there was no retreat. The syrup smell had vanished, and the safety of the parking lot, the darkness hiding our car and the bravado of its passengers, disappeared like smoke.

Adrenaline was now working against me, and the byproduct of adrenaline—urine—was the malady of the moment. I jumped out of the car and ran behind the dumpster. As luck would have it, I'd begun relieving myself just as the cooks were taking the trash out. Out of habit, I looked at my watch. It was just about the same time we took the trash out back at Key West. The cooks looked at me, mumbled something, and laughed as they walked off. They obviously didn't know they were laughing at a real tough guy—a kingpin who'd just passed off a lucrative deal.

When I got back to the car, I did my best to demonstrate

how prepared I was for that moment. "Okay, let's get going. Do the speed limit and no radio."

I made the call to the boss. "We're on our way home."

"Call every thirty minutes," my dad's voice replied. "Be safe."

The option to "be safe" had gone out the window about fifteen minutes ago.

The Power of Self-Deception

As I look back now, I find it strange that the thoughts of pancakes and fears of failure overcame worry over my family. After all, I was doing it all for my family.

But I was overcome with pride and greed. Yeah, I was nervous. But in my heart, my pride had collided with insanity, and the byproduct was self-deception. And there is no worse deception than self-deception.

I'd deceived many people over the years, but the most pain has always come from self-deception. I've found that self-deception leads to the abuse of others. I could only see the world through my own feelings. And a life focused on feelings can quickly spiral out of control. Feelings can guide you, sure, but they can't be your map.

I hadn't yet become a believer, so I didn't understand yet that feelings acted upon without Christ can get you in deep water. When the starting point involves no relationship with Christ, it's all downhill from there. The devil is a master of inverting things. Before you know it, up is down and down is up.

So, there I was, risking my freedom, my family, and maybe even my life. My reputation in Key West was good, but I was about to reveal my true character and assault my reputation with impunity and yet I was getting pumped up, truly feeling like my value was on the rise.

Is that not the world we live in? The good seems bad and the bad seems good. With no firm foundation, no guiding standard, we rely on our own autonomy. And we're quick to justify unjust behavior. Sin breeds complacency, conformity, and compromise.

As I look back, I see God's grace at work. I could have seized that moment of hesitation —an extension of grace. All I had to do was stop for a moment. However, without the infilling of the Holy Spirit, my only moral guide was myself. I was governed by my own law. The law of the flesh. And my flesh wanted complacency and conformity far more than conscience and Christ. Self-deception at work, time and time again.

Why ignore such common sense? Well, that's because that's all I had—my own sense, my own standards. As I have learned, the best that man has to offer is only the best that man has to offer.

Rolling the Dice

I once knew a guy who always dreamed of putting a million bucks on the craps table and rolling the dice, just one time. I told him he was an idiot. "Give me the money," I told him, "and I'll make sure you're entertained often."

But now, looking back, I wonder who the idiot really was. I had rolled the dice on my wife, my children, my family, my freedom, my memories, my future—all in one roll. I had rolled the dice on things that are priceless. Heck, I had a good job in Key West. I worked a lot, and that Key West restaurant was a challenge. But it was good. It was just going to be a long process to develop success. The problem was, I really did not know how to define success. My good friend and mentor

Dwight Bain says, "The first success is to define what success means to you."

My definition of success was tied to two things only: money and my dad's approval.

Our costs at the restaurant were outrageous. It was almost impossible to make any money there without record sales each week. The restaurant became a place of anxiety for me. My contentment and peace were tied to the ebb and flow of the restaurant's business and my father's opinion. Even when we won restaurant of the year in 1993, beating out nearly 500 other businesses, I still never felt success there.

Now I've learned that when your definition of peace is skewed, so is your path to finding it. I loved the business. I loved interacting with different people each day and the busyness of a crowded restaurant. It was a place where I was in control, and quite frankly, I was good at the people and food business. But I never experienced satisfaction or completeness there, no matter how hard I worked. I would have moments when I felt like I had finally climbed that ladder, but nothing I found or experienced had any sustaining power.

By 1994 I was tired of working so hard and not producing any profits. Dad was tired of it, too. And although it was his money that had built the place, I felt the impact of the failure deep in my soul far more than he ever dreamed. He made sure to constantly remind me. It was a perfect setup for what came next.

The Trip Home

The trip home from Miami seemed to take eight hours, though it was actually just a three-hour drive. It was long and tedious. After all, trying to maintain the perfect speed limit, not too fast and not too slow, was difficult even for a gangster. It had

taken 30 minutes to find a place I felt was secure enough to
get out of the car and stow the backpack in the trunk, under
the spare tire. It was amazing how four pounds weighed my
trunk down, like I was driving a lowrider.

"I'm supposed to be tougher than this," I scolded myself. I
didn't want my buddy, eight years my junior, to know I was
scared.

As darkness settled in, every car in my rearview started to
look like a cop car. I felt like I must have seen dozens before
arriving home. The boss called every twenty minutes to see
where his package was. Or maybe to see where we were—after all, we were the package.

I was owned by this harlot—a true 2-for-1 deal. Where
I went, so did the four pounds of theft, robbery, addiction,
adultery, lying, and destruction. We were in the business
of low morality, and we always succeeded at lowering the
standards.

When we pulled up to my house on Sugarloaf Key, my buddy jumped out and got into his own car. "Let me know when
we go again," he said, before driving off.

When he pulled away, I walked out onto my dock overlook-
ing the canal. The night was suddenly eerily quiet. I could
hear the chatter of a TV and the neighbors' laughter floating
from a house across the water. I looked at the moon reflecting
on the water—so clear, so still, so inviting. I loved getting in
the water there. I often found crawfish—the Florida lobster—
underneath the dock. My son loved to see Daddy in the water, and he would join me with his water wings on. So young
and tender, he was just a sponge absorbing everything Daddy
had to say. He watched everything I did. I loved being in that
water, laughing along with him.

But at this moment, I was not laughing. I was nervous. I had
brought a harlot, a killer back home with me. I got up and

walked back to the carport. I opened up an outside closet, pushing aside fishing poles, strollers, toys—everything else a dad might keep in a garage closet, everything that pointed to family and unity—and stashed the package inside. Then, as casually as I could, I walked in the back door and got ready for bed.

Around midnight, I woke up for the tenth time. My wife and my son were sound asleep. I looked out the window, just waiting for something to arrive. I wasn't sure what. Restless, I got up and took my Smith & Wesson 45 out of the closet and put it next to my bed. Not enough. I went out into the kitchen. I placed a Smith & Wesson 357 L-frame by the back door and a shotgun in the pantry. *Good thing I'm not nervous.*

At 7 a.m. the next morning, a Cessna 172 took me to Panama City. It was a four-hour flight, and the views were great. When we landed, I met the boss in the bathroom of a tiny Fixed Base Operation air terminal, which is a place for non-commercial private aircraft, and handed over the 4.4 pounds of anxiety. Then we parted ways. The boss was leaving right away for Country Music USA—he would be bringing a "lady" home. With the weight off my shoulders, I found a chicken wing sanctuary and ordered three times what I needed. After all, I could.

I made two bills that first trip—two grand. I always made *bills,* not *bucks.* Two bucks meant two hundred.

I headed home. Four days later, we were back in business. This time I needed 3 kilos. Why not? If I made it count, I'd grow the business.

It got easier. What started as an anxiety trip soon became the sedative that blocked out all the other pain. When business was good, everything else lost its importance. The restaurant, the failures, the disappointment—I could hide it all in that backpack.

Last Days

May 1997 was a slow period for us. The price of cocaine in Miami was skyrocketing, and availability was limited. Usually when this happened, it meant that someone decided they wanted more money for their product. Simple supply and demand economics at work. The product was available—it was always available—but the price was always changing. The folks in Nashville started complaining about the prices as well, so we started purchasing smaller quantities.

I'd just made a trip to Nashville to drop off a delivery the day before when I got a call. There seemed to be a problem with the quality of several of the packages. I called the folks in Miami to register my concern.

"No problem. We'll swap it out," they replied. So, we arranged a trip the next week to swap out a few packages.

Two weeks later, I got a text from my dad on my pager. *30*17*21.* By then I knew well what that meant: he wanted 30 kilos, he was willing to pay $17,000 each, and delivery was to be on the 21st. It was a rather large order. I sent a message to the folks in Miami and waited for a reply. There were some negotiations, like usual, but we settled on the price and the date was set.

On delivery day, I caught a small private plane to Miami, bringing the money in duffle bags. When I landed, I rented a car and beeped my Miami connection, Ralph, letting him know I was in town. He gave me a call and told me to pick him up at a restaurant on 26th street.

The process went down as it always did. After picking him up, we drove around for 30 minutes or so until he felt comfortable. Then he directed me to a subdivision, where we pulled into the driveway of a house. It was the kind of house you would see when the realtor was advertising a family-friendly neighborhood.

We took the money inside and counted the bundles. The money was banded together the same way each time: 100's in ten-thousand-dollar stacks grouped together to make $100k, 50's in five-thousand-dollar stacks grouped together to make $50k, and 20's grouped together in two-thousand-dollar stacks grouped together to make $20k. It never took too long to count the money.

Next, we left the money on the table and got back in the car. The money and the drugs were never in the same location—if a bust goes down, you don't want to lose the product and the cash. We drove for another 30 minutes or so, eventually pulling into another neighborhood and into the driveway of another all-American house. I backed into the driveway and Ralph got out. About two minutes later, he was back and placed the package in the trunk.

We'd done this enough that I knew the rhythm. Once the package was in the trunk, Ralph would bid me goodbye and say he hoped to see me again. He would *never* get back in the car once the package was in the trunk. He would not take the risk of getting caught. In over three years, he had never come close to doing anything of the sort.

I was getting ready to pull out of the driveway when Ralph stopped me. He asked if I could wait a second, as he needed to get something, and wondered if I could drop him back off at his car.

Alarm bells were blaring in my head. This could not be good. I had always trusted Ralph, but then again, there really was no honor among thieves. I didn't know what to think. I just nodded.

As Ralph walked back into the garage, I took my Smith & Wesson 45 out from under my seat and moved it to the slot between myself and the door, making it quickly accessible by my left hand.

Ralph got in the car and we started driving down SW 8th Street. After a few minutes, he broke the silence.

"Mikey, the cocaine is no good," he said in his Cuban accent.

I remembered the problem from two weeks ago, and the difficulty with the return and exchange of the product. "Hey, we can't have any more problems with the quality," I said.

"The yayo is perfect," Ralph replied—yayo being slang for cocaine—"but you know what I think?"

I couldn't fathom what he might have been thinking, or what he was about to say.

Ralph leaned forward and pointed up toward the sky. "I don't think God likes people selling cocaine."

My head was spinning, thoughts racing. Ralph and I had done every deal together. He could not be saying this. After all, he had to be as greedy and blind as I was.

Ralph didn't know that I had been hanging out with Christian men for a few years. I'd even gone to Bible studies at their houses. I'd started to love these men whose lives absolutely fascinated me. They were so sure of themselves, yet so humble. They were loyal husbands, and they seemed to practice what they preached. I loved being around them— that just wasn't my lifestyle. I was drinking, drugging, and selling millions of dollars of cocaine.

As I was driving, my life was flashing before my eyes: my family, my children, the memories of everything I had heard about God. Hundreds of thoughts filled my mind with complete clarity in just a few seconds.

"What do you mean?" I finally asked Ralph.

"Mikey, Jesus Christ no like cocaine," he replied in his thick Cuban accent. "After today, me no more. My heart is now for Jesus."

We were quiet. Neither of us said a word for the rest of the drive.

Finally, I pulled up to his car. He opened the passenger door, got out, and looked back at me. "Mikey, be careful. I will pray for you."

"Pray for me?" We did not pray for one another. We bought and sold cocaine together. We went to strip clubs together. I felt numb.

The drive to the Ft. Lauderdale FBO felt like it took twice as long as usual. My dad called on the way—I lied and told him I was stopping for food. In reality, I just couldn't talk.

I felt convicted. When I got on the plane, I prayed. I asked to be delivered from this greed machine that had me in its clutches. I wanted to stop, but I did not know how to tell my dad. I was still worried about the wrong father. I had found my personal value in selling cocaine and pleasing my dad.

I told him I wanted to take a break and focus on the restaurant for a couple of months. We could continue what we were doing for now; just with someone else. So someone else filled my shoes. I never flew to Nashville again, never went to Miami to see Ralph again.

On August 15th, 1997, the Drug Enforcement Administration (DEA) started arresting folks in Nashville. I'll leave out the details, as I certainly do not want to glorify anything we did. But on that day, my world began to unravel. However, peace was on its way to my heart. Peace would arrive on September 6th.

Reflection Questions

1. In what ways might you be deceiving yourself in your life? What pain has it caused for yourself and others?

2. What olive branch of grace might God be offering you right now? What might accepting it look like?

3. What does success look like to you right now? Does your definition need to shift?

2

PROMISED LAND DEFINED

Turning Around

The story of the Nashville drug bust had already made the headlines in the local Key West newspaper. Headlines stated, "Local Restaurant Owner Involved in Cocaine Conspiracy." It was shocking and devastating news to my wife, my family, and my friends.

On Friday, September 6th, I called my mentor Len Rogers and asked him if he could come over to my house. Len was a fisherman; he and his wife Virginia moved to the Keys to fish

and help start a church. If there was one man on this planet who I would listen to, it was Len.

Len said he had been expecting my call. I will never forget his first words to me then: "I love you, but now I know why you have been acting like a jacka-- for the last three years."

When he showed up at my house, I began to empty my conscience. We talked, I listened, and I confessed my sins. It was a general list, as we did not have days and days to sit and talk. I told him about the cocaine trafficking and the partnering lifestyle. Then, abruptly, and with a heavy dose of ignorance and arrogance, I told him I wanted to rededicate my life to Christ. Surely, a rededication would clean my conscience. Then again, deep down, I also wondered if God could deal with the consequences of my actions.

Of course, God can do that. But many times, the problem with our confession is that it is bathed in sorrow not over what has been done, but over having been caught. Relationship with God is left out of our feelings of remorse.

Yes, I'd wanted to quit right after Ralph spoke to me a few weeks earlier. I felt convicted. But I was waiting to exit on my own terms. You know, the slow fade into sin retirement. Let us be thankful that God does not let us simply retire sins—otherwise there would be too many coming back out of retirement. No, God seeks to destroy the sin in our lives completely.

Len grinned. "Mike, you can't redo something that has never been done the first time. Christ is not at the center of your heart."

He was right. My ego was in the way. And E.G.O., as my friend Dwight Bain states, "Edges God Out." God was absent in my heart because I didn't make room for Him.

I had always lived for the moment; immediate gratification ruled my life. Months later, my prison counselor would tell me, "This is your problem: you're a P.I.G." In response to my confusion, he continued, "You have a Problem with Immediate Gratification." I'd wanted pleasure, power, and position immediately, and now I was hoping for restoration immediately. I wanted something new and shiny from that day forward, but my restoration was not focused on my wife, family, friends, co-workers, or God. Thus, I was not prepared for what God would take me through to draw me unto Himself and bring healing in my relationships.

Restoration has two sides: the repentance side toward God and the consequence side toward family, friends, and society. I had hoped that God's plan for molding, shaping, and disciplining His children would be accomplished in my life in the same way a grandparent scolds their grandchild—not too harshly. I was looking forward to receiving my easy button—or, at the very least, a semi-easy button.

I never received it, and I'm betting you haven't, either. I would come to learn the truth of how a loving God works in our lives. We may think our sin is hidden, stowed away in a garage shed or in a duffel bag in the trunk. But in reality, everything we think and do might as well be on the big screen and playing through a bullhorn in God's house. He knows how you have been living and where your heart is focused. I had not fooled God. Sure, I had showed up at church from time to time and even given some money. Just like so many, I was checking off boxes, but accomplishing little more than soothing my conscience.

I knew Len was correct; my heart had never belonged to God. So, Len took me through the collection of verses known as the Romans Road to Salvation. These are a collection of verses from the book of Romans that map out the journey to God's salvation (Romans 3:23, 5:8, 6:23, 10:9, 10:13). When strung together, they read like this:

For all have sinned and fall short of the glory of God. But God demonstrates His own love toward us, in that while we were still sinners, Christ died for us. For the wages of sin is death, but the gracious gift of God is eternal life in Christ Jesus our Lord. ... If you confess with your mouth Jesus as Lord, and believe in your heart that God raised Him from the dead, you will be saved. For "Everyone who calls on the name of the Lord will be saved."

I had heard all of these verses before, but I had lived a life that mocked the truths of those divine words. My tears began to flow. I was so full of stress and anxiety. I knew I was broken. I was broken before God and for God.

With my wife and children in the other room, I got down on my knees and confessed my sins, inviting Christ into my life. After my prayer, I stood up and turned to Len. "Well, I sure don't understand how God works, but I can tell you that something has just happened."

Something indeed did happen. My heart felt different, but I couldn't quite make sense of what I had felt. Though I did not understand at the time, I would later find my explanation in scripture. Ephesians 1:13–14 says, *"In Him, you also, after listening to the message of truth, the gospel of your salvation— having also believed, you were sealed in Him with the Holy Spirit of the promise, who is a first installment of our inheritance, in regard to the redemption of God's own possession, to the praise of His glory."*

When I invited the Lord into my life, I was sealed with His Holy Spirit.

Not only that, but I was also positionally seated in Heavenly Places as stated in Ephesians 2:4–6: *"But God, being rich in mercy, because of His great love with which He loved us, even when we were dead in our wrongdoings, made us alive together with Christ (by grace you have been saved), and raised us up with Him, and seated us with Him in the heavenly places in Christ Jesus."*

These promises are part of the promised land of the scriptures. It would be on these two truths that I would rest from that day onward. My position in Christ was *secured.* This has been monumental in my walk, as it led me to the discovery of my value.

We all want to feel valuable, and I knew that a two-time felon might have difficulty finding acceptance and value in society. And that is okay. I get it. I have never tried to argue away someone's opinion about my past because I am now a follower of Christ. Nope, I have earned those earthly consequences. But a constant reflection on those two truths and who Christ is has set me free. It has brought mending to relationships I thought were unrepairable.

You see, if a believer forgets who he is in Christ, he will always act and feel like something he is not.

Once salvation is secured, then comes the hard part: the sanctification process—the process of being shaped into Christ's image. This is God's work in our life while we are on earth. We are justified at salvation, glorified at death, and between the two, we are being sanctified. The awesomeness of God's continued sanctification work in our lives proves that we do belong to Him. Check out this wonderful promise in Hebrews 2:11: *"For both He who sanctifies and those who are sanctified are all from one Father; for this reason, He is not ashamed to call them* brothers and sisters ... "

The first part was not difficult, for the full weight of that moment was borne by Christ as explained in 1 Peter 2:24: *"and He Himself brought our sins in His body up on the cross, so that we might die to sin and live for righteousness; by His wounds you were healed."* So, it is my belief in His finished work at the cross, death, burial, and resurrection that had positioned me in Him.

The second part, however, is not so easy. Ever since that moment, I have continuously learned that God will use the most unorthodox methods to shape His children in His Son's image. God's work in my life has included prison, unemployment, brokenness, failure, defeats, and struggle, as well as success and victory. The Christian life is sometimes called the upside-down life: you must be lost to be saved, you must be last to be first, and tithing 10 percent goes farther than the 90 percent you kept behind. None of that makes sense to someone who hasn't experienced the Christian life for himself.

But do not fear. Whatever you bring to the table, God will work with it. God's methods are unorthodox because we bring Him such a mess. I want you to hear this truth from Romans 8:28: *"And we know that God causes all things to work together for good to those who love God, to those who are called according to His purpose."*

It is important to note that God does not take a bad thing and make it a good thing. Selling cocaine, living for pleasure, and mocking God will always be bad. But God can take those ingredients, work with them, add in some other flavors, and produce something beautiful.

Unorthodox Methods

The nation of Judah certainly knew of God's unorthodox methods. Do you remember Habakkuk? He was an Old Testament prophet, who was the last prophet sent to Judah before its fall into Babylonian captivity. He liked to argue with God. The reason? God's methods seemed unfair and unjust. Judah's morality had vanished, and sin and idolatry were rampant. King Josiah had died, and the nation was soon to be judged. Habakkuk pleaded before God and asked that He would bring an end to the wickedness—the wickedness of God's own chosen people.

Habakkuk pleaded, *"Why do You make me see disaster, And make me look at destitution? Yes, devastation and violence are before me; Strife exists and contention arises,"* (Habakkuk 1:3).

Habakkuk's plea was for God to intervene and convert those sinners in Judah. Undoubtedly, God could orchestrate events to garner an immediate heart change. But He chose to allow it to be a process. It is in the process that we learn a new way to live and a hatred for the old life. There's no waving of a magic wand; instead, God goes to work.

Look at God's answer to Habakkuk: *"Look among the nations! Watch! Be horrified! Be frightened speechless! For I am accomplishing a work in your days—You would not believe it even if you were told. For behold, I am raising up the Chaldeans, That grim and impetuous people Who march throughout the earth To take possession of dwelling places that are not theirs,"* (Habakkuk 1:5-6).

That was a head-scratcher for me the first several times I read it, as well as other like verses. *Let me get this straight ... God is going to deal with His disobedient children by bringing up the Babylonians to conquer them, disperse them, and bring them into slavery?* Yep, that's it. God would raise up the Babylonians to do His work in His children. The brokenness and sin in my life and Judah's could not be addressed through our own designs and discipline.

Where the rubber meets the road, it is simple: a broken hammer cannot fix a broken hammer. We need someone outside of ourselves to bring a change, and when we are ready to allow God to work, He has someone or something on deck divinely prepared. Here is the wonderment of His work, because God cannot look upon our sin nor will He partner with sin. He works on His children because of His nature, because of who He is and His promises, and because Christ lives in our hearts. It is not because we are craving His work; we like sin too much. Rather, it's because of His faithfulness to Himself.

As God has worked to mold and unfold my life, His plan has been an imaginative work that Hollywood could never conceptualize. Thus, the truth of Habakkuk 2:4b: "… the righteous one will live by his faith" has become the rallying cry of those whom God loves.

In the end, Habakkuk writes these words: "Even if the fig tree does not blossom, And there is no fruit on the vines, If the yield of the olive fails, And the fields produce no food, Even if the flock disappears from the fold, And there are no cattle in the stalls, Yet I will triumph in the Lord, I will rejoice in the God of my salvation" (Habakkuk 3:17–18). He realized that, though things weren't looking good, his confidence was in God and His plan.

The Promised Land

After my confession, prayer, and a bit more talking, Len taught me a new phrase: "The Promised Land." As we were standing in the driveway, he asked me, "Well, Mike, you've been searching your whole life for the Promised Land—what have you found?"

I told him I had been all over the country and seen some great places I'd thought about moving someday. I knew I needed to get out of South Florida. I wanted to believe he was referring to the right place to settle down: the right city, the right state. But then I knew better. He was not talking about occupying a piece of land; rather, he was speaking of the occupancy of my heart.

Just what was my heart's desire? So far, it had been anything and everything except for Christ. Saint Augustine so beautifully and accurately stated in his Confessions, "You have made us for Yourself, O Lord, and our heart is restless until it rests in You."[1] That was far from where my heart was. What was I pursuing with such zeal and reckless abandon? (You'll read more about it later in this book.)

Len explained that "the Promised Land is the place where you have quit searching, your heart is full and settled in Christ, and you know it." I wasn't yet sure what Len was referring to, but I knew I was going to find out.

Ask yourself, "What occupies the center of my heart?" Today, I am disgusted when I look back on how arrogant, how untouchable, how lofty in attitude and actions, how selfish I was. Other people might have looked at me and said, "Mike's a good guy; he's not hurting anyone." But that was a lie. I was a wolf dressed up in sheep's clothing.

Len was correct. I was after the "pie in the sky." Merriam Webster defines the phrase as, "an unrealistic enterprise or prospect of prosperity."[2] Every place I had searched was unrealistic in its ability to fulfill my heart. In the end, I found no lasting prosperity anywhere. But boy, was I a "pie-eater." And I liked just about every flavor. My heart was a devourer of pleasure. I had been looking for pleasure instead of promises.

The Struggles We Share

During the last eight years as the Men's Ministry leader at our church and in my work at the Union Mission, I have learned that men do not struggle so differently from each other, regardless of our varying backgrounds. We have a lot more in common than we admit. The essence of the issue is simply that Christian men still struggle with temptation, meaning, and purpose. There is a constant pursuit of another "Promised Land" in each man's heart. I have learned that God never makes peace with our flesh. The flesh is not redeemed, and the devil and his minions are just doing push-ups, ready to go at any moment.

To be honest, I am much better equipped to comment on all the places where the "Promised Land" is *not* found than to write about the true Promised Land. But the Lord has opened my eyes in each area to reveal His way and His Promised Land promises. Remember, whatever God takes away, He replaces with something wonderful.

My initial fears as a Christian largely revolved around areas of sin that needed to be removed but had brought something to my life, whether it was comfort, acceptance, or misplaced value. I had found something I needed. There is nothing wrong with wanting comfort, acceptance, and value; it just needs to be attained God's way. God never rips one leg off the four-legged chair so you have to strain to keep balanced. No, He replaces the leg.

In this book, you will read of the contrast between "pie in the sky" and the fruit of the Promised Land. If you will be honest with yourself, I believe you will see yourself in these chapters.

I will let you in on the secret as to why I believe this: I have spoken and shared my testimony in many settings, and I am always able to keep my audience's attention. But really, all I do is preach to myself. I have spoken of my struggles and sin past and present, as well as Christ's victories through me. I find that so few Christian men are willing to share their life. If Christianity was a sport, it would be the only one in which the victor did not speak of his victories. I've found that when I preach to me, it resonates with men of all backgrounds. My walk with Christ has been thrilling, exciting, difficult, sinful, and painful, but it has never been lonely.

Just as Len explained, I have quit searching. I am still in progress, but I am full and settled, and I know it.

It is important to note that each chapter does not represent a Promised Land that sits alone. There was not a progression from one to the next, leaving behind ones that have been "completed." Rather, there was a co-mingling of these areas. For there are only two places to stand in life: with Christ or away from Christ. There is no no-man's-land for the undecided.

My prison counselor once told me "Hardy, you have to decide if you are going to live by God's standard or the world's standard." The world's standard—the area outside of Christ—encompasses all 57 million square miles of this world. Compare that to the place where we stand *with* Christ: 5.5"x3.5"x2.5"—the size of a human heart. No comparison, right?

Yet the heart that has entered God's Promised Land contains the very One who created the 57 million square miles, and He owns it all. It is the heart that holds the One who provides every provision a person could need both on earth and in heaven.

As you read, you will see that these areas outside of Christ built upon each other, leaned on each other, and fed each other in my life. Sin only feeds sin. In the end, I found myself standing in a barren wilderness, and I was starving. There is only one dish served in the world's Promised Land, and I had eaten all the "pie in the sky" it had to offer. Yet I was empty. I hope that, in reading these next few chapters, you will find yourself in at least one of them. And I hope that, with Christ, you can remove that pie from your diet.

Reflection Questions

1. Can you pinpoint the moment you surrendered your heart to Christ? You may not remember the exact date and time, but do you remember that moment?

2. If your thoughts and actions were playing on the big screen in God's house, what would it be showing? How do you feel knowing that God is watching?

3. Where do you feel your value lies? Do you need to shift where you find that self-worth?

4. What occupies the center of your heart? Be honest. Remember that it is possible to love God and not have Him at the center of your life.

5. Are you afraid to give up something, thinking you will have to balance on a three-legged chair for the rest of your life? What do you need to give to God today?

6. Where is your Promised Land? What are you searching for?

7. What promise from God are you standing on, trusting, and hoping in today?

3

PASSION DEFINED

The Hidden Hook

I had always been passionate about having a good time. I mean, who doesn't like a good time? I know Nike came out with the phrase "Just Do It" in 1988, but I had been practicing that slogan for a decade by then. Live for the moment, do what you want, and try not to hurt anybody along the way. For many years, that formula worked. But Satan knows how to bait the hook.

Fishermen in the Keys will tell you it is important to hide

the hook in the bait, but not too deep in the bait or it becomes harder to hook your fish. That's because, once you've hooked a fish, you must pull the line hard enough to pull the hook through the bait as well as the fish's mouth. The bait is there, but if you look closely, you will see the hook.

There were times when I was watching Len fish for yellowtail snapper that he would chum the waters and get the fish in such a feeding frenzy that he could clip the bar off the hook and simply cast the barbless hook. The fish would bite, no bait required. He would then lift the line into the boat, give it a shake over his holding tank, and the fish would simply fall off. The fish had such a passion for chum that they would bite at anything.

That's what the world does to us today. It hides the barbless hook amidst a swarm of distraction. The flesh will bite at anything in this world, and the Christ-less heart is vulnerable to the wiles of Satan perpetually. The world hides the hook in an endless variety of things; every TV commercial, magazine, and online advertisement paints a bleak picture of life without their product. Masterfully, advertisers find the right person for each company to demonstrate a passion for their product. They flash bold letters stating, "Get it while you can! It may be gone tomorrow!" It has always seemed strange to me that something so life-changing would be in such short supply.

Each news channel has its own hidden hooks. It chums the waters with its own version of the news to cater to the taste of its listening audience, ultimately working them into a passion that keeps them coming back. Why do they do this? The number one reason is to make money. They sell advertising, which in turn tells you ten other things you need to find happiness.

The world works 24/7 to create new passions to feed us.

Passion Misplaced

Passion, defined by Merriam Webster, is "a strong liking or desire for or devotion to some activity, object, or concept."[3] I used to have my own definition for passion: "anything that makes my flesh feel good." I might not have said it in those exact words, but it was how I lived. Anything that just kept giving was good, and when it ran out, I moved on to something else. It was all a chase for the next flavor of "pie in the sky."

Amazing how, looking back, I see that pattern over and over again throughout my life. First, you feel empty. Then you seek, you enjoy, you fill up. Enjoyment fades, and you feel empty again.

So you repeat, always seeking. Jack Nicholson said it best: "My motto is: more good times."[4] Remember that bumper sticker that used to be plastered everywhere? "Who dies with the most toys wins." The world's system preaches "more" with no eternity in sight.

Now, don't close the book and relegate me to curmudgeon status yet. You will see as you flip these pages that you are not going to read about how some "sinner who found Jesus" (when, in fact, He chooses us) has turned his life around and is now against anything that might make someone smile. I am not against having a good time. I am all for a great time. I am all about passion, but passion must be pursued and applied correctly.

I am all for enjoying life to the fullest—but not my fullest. I want the Lord's fullest. My family and I still treat ourselves well, but I recognize every moment, every pleasure as a God-provided enjoyment.

Len once told me, "The Bible is not a book listing off

restrictions, but rather a book offering protection." Keep that in mind and swallow that truth every day.

I haven't taken a vow of poverty in any sense; I just have a different view now. I am on guard against having a wrong heart. The wrong heart drives passion that creates actions as healthy as water from a farmland stagnant pond. The wrong heart says, "It's all about me."

I remember when I first picked up *The Purpose Driven Life* by Rick Warren and read the first line: "It's not about you."[5] He is exactly right—not because I say so, but because God says so.

What Does "Good" Mean?

Your definition of good is critical to your walk with the Lord. My mantra had always been "Live for the moment, be good to others—or should I say, be good to those who are good to you. And have a good time." I mean, why not? Everyone else is doing it. But that is a lie from Satan.

Whenever you hear someone say, "Everyone else is doing it," remember what your mom told you: "No, they're not," often followed by, "If they jumped off a bridge, would you?"

My dad told me several times about what he thought about God and a relationship with Him. He would say, "God loves us, and He wants us to be good to each other." We often preach what we do not practice. His definition of "good" was skewed in that it excluded God.

Paul records God's observation and truth about man in Romans 3:12: *"They have all turned aside, together they have become corrupt; there is no one who does good, there is not even one."*

Ouch. That busts a lot of balloons.

Further evidence regarding man's use of the word "good"

is found in the story of Lot, as he entertains the two angels God sent to Sodom and Gomorrah, found in Genesis 19. God had judged the two cities, and the angels were there to simply confirm and complete God's previous judgment. Lot greets the angels, disguised as men, and brings them to his house.

The perverted men of Sodom circle Lot's house, attempting to lure the men outside so that they "may know them." That is Old Testament language for engaging in sexual relations. Lot pleads that the Sodomites leave the men alone, and he makes an astonishing offer in Genesis 19:8 (KJV): *"Behold now, I have two daughters which have not known man; let me, I pray you, bring them out unto you, and do ye to them as is good in your eyes: only unto these men do nothing; for therefore came they under the shadow of my roof."*

Are you kidding me? Offer up your daughters to a group of perverted men and tell them to do "good" as they see fit? Let me tell you something; their "good" was evil. "Do ye to them as is good in your own eyes," pretty much sums up the world's system today.

By the way, God sovereignly saves the daughters and the angels. Good and passion is all relative, all autonomous, "to each his own" is the rally cry. I understand; I used to believe and think that way.

So what is passion and good apart from Christ?

Do non-Christians have fun and do good? Absolutely they do. The atheist enjoys a good time and performs good deeds. I have friends and relatives who will give you the shirt off their back, cook your food when you are sick, lend you money when you need it, and listen when you need to talk, and they don't believe in Christ any more than they believe in the man on the moon. Many of them are absolutely wonderful people who are using all their gifts and talents for earthly work. But sadly, there is not an eternity in sight.

Here is what I did not understand before: apart from a relationship with Christ, all one can enjoy and do is limited to the enjoyment that only man can provide. All pleasure touches the heart, and without Christ ruling there, all pleasure is limited in its sustainability. Simply put, we can only enjoy so much without Christ as our influence.

God is simply not going to allow us to enjoy the pleasures of life to their fullest without Him, as He will not allow the world to deliver anything on the level upon which only He can provide.

So we come back to the question, what is passion and good without Christ? It is man's pursuit of pleasure and good that ignorantly settles for less than best. It has a beginning and definite ending; it is a finite behavior.

Think about it. Passion, in its simplest terms, involves three components: the driving force, the object of the passion, and the payoff. Thus, without Christ, the best man can offer is simply the best man can offer. So without Christ, it is only a "pie in the sky," for it cannot deliver anything beyond our grave. You will read in the following chapters how the Lord taught me a new understanding of areas that at one time ruled my flesh.

So how do I define "good" today, as a follower of Christ? I keep these words written on my desk. "Any and everything one does with Christ as the preeminent influence in the activity is good and what He has given me to enjoy."

I like how it is written in James 1:17: *"Every good thing given and every perfect gift is from above, coming down from the Father of lights, with whom there is no variation or shifting shadow."* If it is not coming down from God, it is no good, and you should leave it alone.

Len Rogers told me one time, "The grass is greener on

IN PURSUIT OF THE PROMISED LAND

the other side of the fence because that's where it's being watered."

Abundance

In contrast, I had not been passionate for the Lord. He was, at best, on the outer edges of the radar screen. Probably like many of you, I knew God, Jesus, and the Bible just like I knew George Washington had been the first president—it was all just scholastic facts in the brain. I knew of them, but I did not know them. Such a seemingly infinite distance between the brain and the heart.

Rather, I was passionate about one thing: making money. I remember in the spring of 1996, my dad had immense amounts of cash coming in every 12–14 days. It was so much that we hired someone to sort the money, bundle it properly (same denominations together, bills always facing the same way, and three rubber bands), and count it. We used to joke that we needed to open a bank.

But blindness had set in. We had no end in sight and no exit strategy. We were caught in the moment, not thinking about tomorrow, and morality was all absent. Remember what Paul wrote of Satan in 2 Corinthians 4:4: *"in whose case the god of this world has blinded the minds of the unbelieving so that they will not see the light of the gospel of the glory of Christ, who is the image of God."*

Just watch the news. There are plenty of evil things that happen in the dark. In 1996, Dad would pay a pilot to fly money back and forth from Nashville to the Florida Keys. He jokingly referred to me as his storage locker.

Jesus spoke to this type of foolishness in the parable of the rich young fool in Luke 12:16–21. Christ describes a rich man who had an overabundance of crops in his barns. He had so much that he planned to tear down his old barns and build new ones. Evidently, he expanded his wealth and decided he needed to create new hoarding places. We know he found the answer to his problem as the Lord shares the fool's conclusion in verse 19: *"And I will say to myself, 'You have many goods stored up for many years to come; relax, eat, drink, and enjoy yourself!'"*

How many folks are waiting for that retirement day when they can say that? People spend billions on the lottery and in casinos hoping to say that sentence someday. Obviously, this person in this story worked hard, wisely, and diligently. He must have been passionate about his work, for he was wealthy at a time when poverty was the norm.

Now, there is no problem with working hard, building wealth, and retiring. But this man believed he did not need God. Jesus shares a startling truth regarding the man's proclamation of his wealth and ease of life: *"But God said to him, 'You fool! This* very *night your soul is demanded of you; and* as for all *that you have prepared, who will own* it now?' *Such is the one who stores up treasure for himself, and is not rich in relation to God."* (Luke 12:20–21).

Purpose

I had a buddy in Key West who was a devout atheist. He would say, "Even God said, 'Eat, drink, and be merry, for tomorrow you die!'" It seems like every nonbeliever can (loosely) quote Isaiah 22:13. But there is something huge left out of that statement. We may all eat, drink, and die, but then there is the judgment. Satan leaves that truth out of the sentence.

That buddy of mine died in 1999 in a terrible car wreck.

I will always remember my conversations with his mother. She hoped he knew the way of truth ... "He was such a good son." A definitive true statement, but not the one that opens the door to eternal life.

As I look back on my life, I see that I had one rule that was always at work. Rule #1: Place the needs, wants, passions, and desires of Mike before anything else. For that I was passionate. If you had asked me 25 years ago, "What type of guy are you? Where do you place your priorities?" I would have said this:

"Oh, god first," (with a little "g" on purpose), "family, friends, work, others, my dog, my toys," et cetera, et cetera. I would continue, "I am honest, straightforward, friendly, and sure, I may sow some wild seed every so often, but I am not hurting anyone. Ultimately, I like helping others, and I especially enjoy looking after my family."

Wow, what a guy. Who doesn't want that guy as a neighbor or drinking buddy? At first glance, there's nothing inherently wrong about that guy. But you know, when I read that statement, even though I've just written it, I feel like an idiot.

What is your life-defining statement? Take a minute to write it out. And don't just write the statement you're "supposed to" to get your holy card punched. Rather, write the one that most quickly comes to your mind.

As you go through this book, you will see the promises from the Promised Land that help define the believer's life. By the end of the book, you will rewrite your statement. I promise it will look different.

As I reflect on my old life-defining statement, an obvious pattern is revealed. None of my top priorities ever stayed in order. My passion was always moving. I have ascertained this absolute truth: if God's not number one, nothing on the list has any chance of staying in the correct order.

After a lot of reflection, I took the time several years ago to write down a new life-defining statement. Here is what that statement looks like now:

Mike's Life-Defining Statement

LIFE

A life that daily is surrendered to Christ—manifested through an obedient response to the gospels and teachings of Christ. That every area of my life will be under the direct influence of Christ. I want His name, Jesus, to follow any mention of my name, behavior, and actions. To daily partake of God's holy word through reading, prayer, meditation, and listening. To make up my mind each day to serve Christ.

WIFE

To lead my wife as the spiritual, emotional, and physical leader of our home. That my wife would always know my truest and fullest support in all she does and believes. To always have eyes, heart, and desire only for my wife and to never place my wife in a position of insecurity or inferiority to anything or anyone else. That my love for Judy will always glorify Christ and lead my wife to be more like Christ and stronger in every sense in which she seeks my help and aide for strength. To constantly work toward placing her every need before mine—her emotions, interests, dreams, and hopes. Every day is an opportunity to love her, cherish her, enjoy her, and give God thanks for her— to NEVER waste this opportunity.

FAMILY

That my kids, grandkids, and family would know that I love Jesus Christ. To see me as honest, trustworthy, patient and kind, and that they would see Christ as the driving influence in my life's decisions, choices, opinions, and health. They would know me as a go-to reference for help, wisdom, encouragement, and Godly counsel. When I do not know answers, I will help seek answers. That I would always make myself available when I am needed and/or to the best of my ability at the time. That patience and Christlikeness would be the prevailing personality in my life as they seek guidance. To love my family with each opportunity God provides, knowing always that my family is a gift to me from God. In conclusion, I will be generous with my family and others as the Lord provides—knowing all that I have is granted unto me for stewardship, not ownership.

Upon the first read-through, this statement certainly sounds impressive. But I am imperfect, and holding to these standards is something I have to aim for each day. I keep this statement posted on the wall in my office. It is a great daily reminder, especially on days when I am working on getting "back into my coffin", more on this in a bit. (Just now, I asked Judy how I was doing with these goals. She smiled and said, "Remember we operate under grace," then gave me a kiss and walked off. We'll say it's a work in progress.)

Priority

Recently, my friend Dwight shared with me that the word "priority" was originally created to be a singular word. There could only be one priority. *Priorities,* in the plural, became popular in the 1950's as men tried to juggle life, passions, and toys. So it's not so much that I had a wrong list of priorities as it is that I had no singular priority in life. If you place your wife, kids, job, or any passion at #1 and bump God down to #2, your top ten list will eventually look like the numbered balls on the Friday night lotto drawing. Who knows what number will be coming up first?

I know it's hard, especially in relationships. But the hard truth is that your wife cannot be #1 with God #2, or eventually your wife will end up at #7 and God will be out of the top 10 altogether. I have tried, millions of men have tried, and maybe even someone you know has tried. It doesn't work. Be honest with yourself, look around, and the evidence will be overwhelming. Most of us know a guy who is not happy at home. It's possible he tried to keep his wife at #1, but Satan took over the order of priorities.

I thought my old life-defining statement was okay. It's funny how our own autobiographies, without Christ, sugarcoat everything. Every unwritten autobiography is a bestseller. Self-inspection is difficult and rare. We might do an okay job with our clothes before a dinner date, but we're less inclined to examine our own attitudes and hearts with critical eyes. I have learned that I cannot look at self without Christ. My eyes always see self as if I am looking into a mirror. There's nothing wrong with a mirror if you use it the way it is meant to be used. It shows a picture of the outside. And though how we look on the outside may make us feel better, it still does not reveal our heart, emotions, and feelings.

I often tell the men at the Union Mission in Orlando that if I look through the window at other people, I never look too bad. But when I get in front of a mirror, the view changes. Yet mirrors only provide a glimpse of what makes a person. In his poem *Auguries of Innocence,* Poet William Blake wrote:

"This life's dim windows of the soul
Distorts the heavens from pole to pole
And leads you to believe a lie
When you see with, not through, the eye."[6]

My eyes too often are solely connected to my feelings and

not my conscience. Christ sees through us as if we are a window. We need His eyes for inspection. We need to see self through Heaven's lens. Now I approach everything in my life from that perspective. It's how I approach my opinions, especially the political ones. It is through Heaven's eye that we are to view policy, people, and platforms. What does God see?

Pinball

I always liked things that made me feel good and things that made others feel good. Nothing superficially wrong with that. My feelings were important, and I lived, breathed, and operated according to my feelings. It's like that old quote often attributed to Yogi Berra, "Whatever you do, you should do it with feeling."[7]

But I was the pinball in an old 70's arcade machine. I was just a ball rolling around, and I wasn't in control of my direction; I was simply bouncing off in whatever direction the flipper sent me. All my directions were dictated by things outside of me. Left flipper sends you high and to the right, loop around the wire tunnel and ring a few bells, then the mid-left flipper sends you across to the three bullseyes where you score maximum points.

The goal of the game was to keep the ball moving; the direction really did not matter. As you played, you were serenaded by the bells and whistles of the game, hoping to win the prize. Do you remember what the prize was in pinball? It was always an extra ball. You won by keeping the ball in endless sporadic motion. Score enough points, ring enough bells, flash enough lights, and boom, out comes an extra ball. Another chance to score a few points.

If you are not careful, you will find that just like I was, you are a pinball ricocheting through life. It often works like this:

you head into the office in the morning and on the way, some guy nearly runs you off the road. Next thing you know, you are practicing your style of road rage. Or you meet the boss in the parking lot, and he is not too friendly. Suddenly you're upset with the people you work with. If you run into something pleasing, then you're happy; run into something sad, then you're sad. You are pretty much just a puppet dancing on the strings of a puppet master. Puppet masters come in all shapes and sizes.

So my feelings were my guide, my master. And let me tell you, feelings are overrated. Especially in today's world where one person's hurt feelings can impact so many others. We cancel dances, luncheons, parties, and parades because someone somewhere has their feelings hurt.

Please know that I am not suggesting that feelings are not real and important, nor am I suggesting people are not free to feel a certain way about something, or that they should "just get over it" when their feelings are hurt. However, I'm sure our Lord's feelings were hurt, too, but He went to the cross. I am not sure Christians are on solid ground when they voice that they have been offended by someone, because Christ was offended and yet He went to Calvary.

I know we do not have ice water in our veins, and we do experience real feelings and emotions. There is just simply no good guidance that comes from operating solely based on feelings. I want to make this clear; I am speaking of a truth that is irrelevant to our heart's pursuit. However, there are times when feelings should override a truth.

I think back to the times when my kids would ask if their painting was the best I had ever seen; truthfully, probably not, but their feelings were important and my answer was a resounding "Yes!" Or the old joke "Does this dress make me look heavy?" Every man and woman knows how to answer that question. No, I am not saying truth is optional, but the kindness, goodness, and love of our Lord should always be at work.

However, when it comes to filling the heart with a secure purpose and meaning, trusting in feelings will only get you in trouble. Feelings often erroneously build up and tear down. Feelings always find fault in the other guy, and as my friend Deacon Davis says, "God is not working on the other guy."

What's worse is that I encouraged others to follow the destructive, erratic path I was taking. Folks who trusted me, thought I was something different than I was, came to me for advice based on the illusion I had created. The world loves a passionate singer, artist, athlete, actor, and just about anyone else who is "all in" on their focus. Perhaps you are seen as passionate. Remember the three parts: what drives it, what it is focused on, and what payoff you are looking for? Stop for a moment and reflect—how do you use the sphere of influence God has afforded you? Are people grateful they took your advice and followed your example? Does your passion reflect Satan or a Saint?

Before Christ, I misused my sphere of influence. When people came to me for advice, I told them to do what felt good. It was all about feelings. I always wanted everyone to enjoy themselves, and if I could help provide that experience, then I was all in. I would leave the house on Friday night with ten grand in my pocket; there were plenty of people willing to ride on that train.

Satan certainly knows who to prop up. I know why they were duped because I was duped. It is Satan's job to dupe people. Oh my goodness, self-deception is devastating.

The reason helping others feels good is often because you are working on making yourself feel special, accepted, and needed. We want to feel like the big shot. I sure practiced that endlessly. Ultimately, anything that is done to glorify self or is done outside of a relationship with Christ is sin. Romans 14:23c says, *" ... and whatever is not from faith is sin."*

Oh, how many times did I attempt to provide that "feel good" moment for the people around me. But it was always delivered on a boomerang; I wanted something back. I needed something. I was searching for something, but I did not know I was searching. I used to joke and say that I was a scientist and that I was just out doing research. After all, the flesh is an exhaustive study.

I did my "study" in five specific areas. You will see the results of my "research" and the lessons God taught me (and is still teaching me). It is not about discarding passion; rather, it is a redirecting of passion. Remember how Saul became Paul—redirected passion.

Be ready to look for yourself in the narrative. Be honest, open, and transparent before your Lord. Let's look at the five places where the Promised Land is not.

Reflection Questions

1. Where is your passion directed? Where would your spouse or best friend say your passion is directed?

2. What does your top ten list look like? Be honest.

3. Are you the "ball" or the "flipper" in the old pinball game?

4. Which emotional response do you practice that needs to be translated into a truth response?

5. Do you find it easy to self-inspect through window gazing?

6. Can you stand in front of a mirror and ask God to reveal your heart to yourself?

7. How do you influence those around you? Does your presence and advice help or hinder them?

8. What is your life-defining sentence right now? (You will write it again at the end of this book.)

4

WHERE THE PROMISED LAND IS NOT FOUND—PLEASURE

About Pleasure

Pleasure was my "apple pie." My favorite pie. Merriam Webster's dictionary defines pleasure as "a state of gratification, sensual gratification or frivolous amusement."[8] Hard to argue with that definition. There's certainly nothing inherently wrong with it, as it seems to fit my life experiences.

However, pleasure is not something that is found daily. We

have all experienced days, weeks, and even years that were less than gratifying. To state the obvious: life has its ups and downs. We all know that. So, the question arises; can life still be embraced and enjoyed when things are not going so well? Or are we doomed to seasons of depression and difficulty with no exit?

I think we have all been there. We've all experienced a season of hardship in which it seemed the sun never shined. Perhaps your joy is relegated to the ease of the day: no problems at work, no arguing with the spouse, the market is up, and the kids are fine. For me, the pursuit of pleasure was directly commensurate with my life satisfaction score.

I'd like you to focus on the word *pursuit* instead of *pleasure*. It is always the pursuit that provides the most entertainment. The dog loves to chase the car and bark, but when you stop the car, he is puzzled. He tilts his head, as if to ask, "Now what do I do?"

That is how my life worked. If I wanted it, I chased it relentlessly. I loved the pursuit. It seemed that my ability to enjoy the pursuit and the object of the pursuit became less and less. From a bird's eye view, it seemed like the world was mine for the taking and enjoying.

In Shakespeare's 1608 play *The Merry Wives of Windsor,* the character Falstaff states when he is refused even a penny, "Why, then, the world's mine oyster, which I with sword will open!"[9] That famous line has become synonymous with the attitude that says, "I will take what I want." My dad lived that way, I lived that way, and money made sure those things happened. However, even back then, I knew there was a problem. It seemed my ability to enjoy the chase, or even what I had caught, provided diminishing returns. The more passionately I pursued, the emptier I felt.

From the world's perspective, things seemed to be in

perfect alignment for endless pleasure. I had all the toys for making life easy and fun. I had money, new cars, boats, homes, and vacations when and where I wanted. We did everything we could to pursue pleasure. It was nothing to take the Learjet to the Caymans for the afternoon so we could get a great fried conch sandwich, or to fly to our favorite restaurant in some faraway city for dinner. We had flights to Miami from Key West for concerts, sporting events, and dinner. Limos and presidential suites at hotels, room service with obscene amounts of food. We even gave generously: huge, life-changing tips at restaurants, cars for friends, down payments on houses, rents paid, cash gifts to folks ... The list could go on. But all of it, and I mean all of it, was given to feed a pleasure that was insatiable. All of it was sin—even the moments in which people were helped. For, as I stated earlier, anything done for the glory of self rather than God is sin.

It seemed that the more I sought and the more I obtained, the more audacious I became. However, I kept running into a problem: nothing had any durability. Looking back, it is clear how miserable I was. But I kept chasing, trying my best to fill something in my soul.

To the outside world, and to my family and friends, I seemed happy. But on the inside, I was caving and crumbling, held together only by ego, greed, self, and pride. And those four ingredients hold things together about as well as Elmer's glue holds two boulders together. Nothing pursued outside of Christ provides any permanency.

Remember when I said I made "two bills" that first day? I could not believe I had 20 one-hundred-dollar bills in my hand. At the end, I had 500 hundred-dollar bills in my hand every three weeks or so. It was not enough.

The Illusion of Pleasure

We have all experienced the thrill and excitement of a long-anticipated event, only to have it fall flat on the thrill rating. That is what I was experiencing, but could not believe it was an inside problem, a heart problem. No, the problem had to be in what pleasure I was chasing. I simply had not found the right one.

Here is a good illustration. I went to Vegas in 1980 after graduating high school: a graduation trip for me and my stepbrother provided by my mom and stepfather. My stepfather gave us each $150 and told us we could go to the casino. I doled out that $150, one dollar at a time. I tried the craps table with $10, but it disappeared so quickly that it was a one-and-done experience. We stayed in Vegas for three nights and two full days; my $150 lasted into the last hours of our trip as, every now and then, the slots would give me some of my money back.

We had a great time, and it is still a special memory. But I quickly realized that my dreams of striking it rich in Vegas were simply that: dreams. And though I was fascinated by all that I saw, I knew that this was not a place where one gets ahead in life. I'm not sure I couched it in these terms, but looking back, I seemed to have had a sense that all of Vegas was like the Siegfried & Roy show we attended: all an illusion.

That's the thing about pursuing pleasure based solely on the flesh; it is an illusion. We end up chasing things that do not really exist. I remember during my cocaine and crack addiction that a $10 high was as good as it was going to get, but I would spend every dollar I had chasing something better, literally spending hundreds to chase ten dollars. It's the same principle with viewing porn or chasing fantasies about the girl you are not with. You are chasing a figment of your imagination. The one you are looking for never appears, the experience never meets your expectations, the passion never adequately fills the heart. If it did, you would stop, no more research needed. The flesh is never full; it simply wants more.

Fast forward from 1980 to 1996. I was in Vegas, at the same hotel as in 1980: the Flamingo. I was in town for two days, and I had tens of thousands of dollars in my pocket with plenty more stashed away in my room. Selling cocaine provided the cash. I was in Vegas, and I could do just about anything I wanted.

Back in 1980, I was a slots guy, or a $10 craps table bet guy, and I made $150 the last three days. But since then, I had been studying and playing poker, blackjack, and the best way to handle the craps table. Yeah, right. Who believes that?

I had not studied anything other than the few games I'd played and lost. But by then, who cared about losing money? There was always more. At least, that's what my ego and a fancy hotel room had convinced me. I'd already spent more than $150 on the valet and baggage guy. Certainly I knew what I was doing.

The truth was that I'd shown up in Vegas just as green in the gambling arena as I had 16 years earlier. I was just more equipped to lose without caring too much. I was in Vegas to pursue the illusion once again that it was a place where one can find pleasure in the flesh that will endure at least as long as an MLB baseball game.

You have probably heard the advertisement that says, "What happens in Vegas stays in Vegas." It should also state that "What happens in Vegas does not change; it delivers the same results."

Please note that I am not singling out Vegas as the pinnacle of wretchedness; it just happens to be the location of my experience. Over the years, I have known plenty of wonderful

Christians who visited Vegas, took in the sights, food, concerts, and shows, and never compromised their walk with Christ. Bottom line, if Vegas was the problem, then I guess everyone in Vegas would be dealing with the same issues. After giving my life to Christ, I began to learn that stuff really is not the problem in life, but rather how you deal with and approach stuff. And, of course, I came to learn that there is some stuff you simply never need to deal with.

Vegas wasn't the problem; it was what was inside my heart that was the deal breaker. My heart pursued all it knew how to pursue: the flesh. Mike was doing life by himself. And a man left to his own moral standards always pursues life at a standard that is less than what God would set.

I was in Vegas dealing with my lust problem—the lust for constant change, never content. Pleasure seekers look for constant newness, emotional highs, and the drive to always "one up" the previous overrated feeling. The entire weekend was a demonstration of arrogance, ego, and my quest to help provide the payroll for every casino I entered. I did much better in 1980. I remember flying home and thinking "I'll do it differently next time I come out here." I bragged to the people I could about my trip, even lying about some of it. But I was faking my gratification, and yet did not even know it.

The Source of True Satisfaction

The thing about placing a pursuit of pleasure as the driving force in our lives is that it is only able to touch some of the senses, and at best it only breathes on the heart. No fulfillment. It never seems to deliver entirely to our whole person; some area of our life is always left out.

Reflecting on my pursuit of continuing insufficient provisions gave me a clearer understanding of John 4 and Jesus' encounter with the woman at the well, found in verses 1–26. Jesus is headed to Galilee and He stops at a well. At the time, there were three different routes to Galilee from Judea, and His route places Him in this women's path. This is a divine appointment.

Jesus is thirsty, so He asks the nearby Samaritan woman for some water. The woman is bewildered, for no Jew is supposed to speak with a Samaritan woman. However, Jesus begins a dialogue with her. The woman, a sinner, had simply wanted water, a temporary filling of her needs. But Jesus simply and lovingly gets right to the root of her emptiness.

Christ first identifies the problem in verse 13: *"Jesus answered and said to her, 'Everyone who drinks of this water will be thirsty again.'"* Okay, and the grass is green and the sky is blue. We all know that our bodies need water; about 72 hours is the limit one can go without water.

Jesus continues, *"'but whoever drinks of the water that I will give him shall never be thirsty; but the water that I will give him will become in him a fountain of water springing up to eternal life.'"*

I remember when studying this passage years ago, I wrote myself a note that said, "You've been drinking from the wrong well most of your life."

What water is this water Jesus speaks of? We can find glimpses of it all throughout scripture. Look at Jeremiah 2:13, where God denounces His disobedient children, the Jews, for turning their hearts against the "fountain of living water." Water is used symbolically of the Lord. Isaiah 12:2–3 beautifully speaks of our salvation using water symmetrically with our faith in the Lord: *"Behold, God is my salvation, I will trust and not be afraid; For the Lord God is my strength and song And has become my salvation. Therefore, you will joyously draw water From the springs of salvation."* Ezekiel also gives us a powerful image of God's "water" and its power in Ezekiel 36:25–26: *"Then I will sprinkle clean water on you, and you will be clean; I will cleanse you from all your filthiness and from all your idols. Moreover, I will give you a new heart and put a new spirit within you; and I will remove the heart of stone from your flesh and give you a heart of flesh."* God's "water" is symbolic of the Holy Spirit in Isaiah 44:3, as God pours out His comfort on His church: *"For I will pour water on the thirsty land And streams on the dry ground; I will pour out My Spirit on your offspring, And My blessing on your descendants."*

As we continue reading the story of the woman at the well, we find out she had many relationships with men. She had been looking to fill her heart with all the flesh could provide. She was empty and thirsty. The story joyously concludes as she receives the "living water" from Christ. We will meet her in Heaven someday.

And there it is— the secret to living an abundant full life in Christ. You keep drinking from His well.

How about another example? John the apostle makes the same point with a different illustration. In John 15:1–11, he writes that Jesus is the vine and the followers are the branches. I love that, for I think of it just about every time I scrutinize a tree. Out my back window I see a chokecherry tree, with large, long branches on the bottom and small, short branches on the top. It produces small cherries that are inedible— except to the bears. Here is the truth about that tree. Those branches do not struggle, fight, or attempt to manipulate each other to obtain water and nutrients. Nope, they simply stay connected to the trunk. By staying connected they survive, and they each produce chokecherries and leaves. The joy of always knowing the Lord's presence is found in staying connected and drinking His water. We do this by reading the Word. And in those moments, days, and weeks when you are tired, sad, or barely hanging in there, you will know His closeness because your natural default system will be to lean on the Father.

Trading Pleasure for Presence

In my pursuit of pleasure, I soon discovered that a forbidden relationship might soothe physical desires, but it is only momentary. The byproduct of that relationship? It can leave the heart feeling guilty. Drugs and alcohol might temporarily soothe pain, but they leave the soul empty and hurting. The "pleasure first" pursuit will always leave you wanting more and more. And there is always more to pursue; Satan makes sure of that.

I'd like to say that after I gave my life to the Lord, the pursuit of pleasure as a driving force completely vanished. But that would be a lie. However, something did happen on that day.

As I said before, on that day when I got down on my knees, confessed my sins, and asked Christ into my life, I really had no idea what happened in my life spiritually at that moment, but I did know that something had just happened. I was aware of Christ's presence and thus, I began to learn what it meant to live in the light of eternity. My focus began to shift to my Savior and not pleasure.

I have never not known His presence. However, my beginnings in Christ did not represent a flawless Christian. I learned that I was perfect vertically, but horizontally I was a work in process. I have found that repentance is a turning from sin as well as a changing of how we view sin. In repentance, we are learning to view sin as God would see it, not as we do with our rose-colored glasses.

Often it is stated by preachers that repentance is a

180-degree turnaround. I have a problem with that image, because some of my turnaround has been like driving around a huge cul-de-sac; it took a while to get headed the right direction on a consistent basis. But here is the most awesome part of my walk with Christ, and I cannot say it enough: since day one of my surrender to Him, I have never felt alone and not been aware of His presence. Even in my failures since my salvation, I have never not known His presence. Christ has never been absent in revealing Himself. Slowly, the shiny things that had once interested me slowly began to lose their luster. Things that I perceived as necessary and sufficient began to be exposed as weak and insufficient in meeting my needs. Any delving back into these things provided only a guilt and a sense that those things just did not fit anymore.

I began to read the Bible. I fell in love with reading the scriptures and finding God's truths that I could apply to my life. Len did not give me a list of "dos and don'ts" on that day in September 1997. There was no list of things that needed to be removed from my "diet." I knew I had not just signed up for some program where I would check off boxes as I moved toward completion and success. Nope, even though I desperately needed change, a checklist would not have worked for me. Len did not give me a checklist, but he did hand me the Bible which I kept on the coffee table.

There is not a single thing that I quit doing because I said, "I'm a Christian now and I cannot do that." Rather, the more I read God's Word, learned of Christ, and better I saw myself with God's eye, the more things simply lost their interest to me. As I worked through areas such as drinking and lust, I would speak to myself throughout the day saying, "Do not drink. Do not lust. Lord, help me not to do those things." Guess what? That did not work so well. Drinking and lust were simply the symptoms of a greater problem: a heart not fully dedicated to Christ. So after years as a Christian, I changed my prayer focus when dealing with different sins. This became my prayer: "Lord, help me draw closer to You."

When I was in prison, I always, and I mean always, carried around five index cards in my pocket. On each card was written five Bible verses. These were the truths on which I was standing. These were promises that the Lord had made to His children. I was claiming them for myself. I always wrote them out with my own name. If I was dealing with loneliness I would write, " *... behold, I am with you (Mike) always, to the end of the age,*" (Matthew 28:20b) on a card. If I was dealing with anxiety and worry, I would write, *"The steadfast of mind you will keep in perfect peace, Because he (Mike) trusts in You."* (Isaiah 26:3) written on a card. I would change the cards out weekly. I learned to trust and believe the word of God.

Perhaps you struggle with trusting Christ. Here is the good news: the only reason you do not trust Him is because you do not know Him, for if you knew Him, you would know you could trust Him. He is trustworthy. He is waiting on you. So get some index cards and start writing.

Looking in the Mirror

Dwight Bain often reminds me that "self-inspection is expensive because it is so rare." When pleasure is your driving force, self-inspection tends to happen by viewing through a window. There is only a faint shadowy glimpse of self, and that only if the lighting is right. And we all know that when you look through windows, at others, to inspect yourself, you tend to look pretty good. Sometimes we do not look so bad when we can pick and choose who we compare ourselves to. Viewing self by looking through glass windows always leaves room to manipulate the view.

However, self-inspection in a mirror is different. It provides a glimpse of self with no one else in view. But even then, we lie to ourselves, or we are deceived. I cannot tell you how many times I have gotten dressed for a dinner date, checked myself in the mirror, declared myself "looking good," only to then have Judy tell me that those stripes do not go with those pants and so on. Back to my closet I would go. (And by the way, she was always right.)

So we do need help with self-inspection. We need a mirror, but we need a special mirror—one that looks internally, at the heart. Our mirror should be Christ and His Holy Spirit. We are to hold ourselves up to Him; after all, we are made in His image, not the other way around.

Today's culture creates individual gods. People conjure up an image of God that looks like whatever they want to see. This has simply created a culture of window gazing and not mirror inspection. Here is the problem: no one can do their own self-exam. Even my GP doctor goes to a doctor for his physical; he does not examine himself. We need a doctor outside of ourselves. And there is no better doctor than Christ.

Now here is the beauty of looking to Christ as our mirror. When He reveals our flaws, failures, shortcomings, sins, and ugly spots, the Holy Spirit does not bring condemnation. Rather, he brings healing and correcting. Romans 8:1 says, *"Therefore there is now no condemnation at all for those who are in Christ Jesus."* What a beautiful, encouraging promise. The ugliness that the Christ-mirror reveals is met with love and the Holy Spirit's desire to bring healing and cleansing to our life. The Christ-mirror reveals ugliness in the heart, but still sees you as one created in His image. I am still fascinated, blown away, by how the Holy Spirit can convict me and reveal to me ugliness, yet I never feel less loved. Rather, I know I am loved deeply and closer to Christ. For 1 John 1:9 says, *"If we confess our sins, He is faithful and righteous, so that He will forgive us our sins and cleanse us from all unrighteousness."*

We are never made cleaner by comparing ourselves to someone else's dirt. I visited my dad in prison for years as he was moved around the country. So many times our conversation would contain fifteen minutes or so of pontificating about how bad some of the other men were that were in prison with him. He was not "near what they were." He never did come to terms with the heinous nature of our actions. Without Christ in our lives, we never see ourselves as filthy as we are. Bottom line, if you are dirty, you are dirty, no matter what pigpen the other guy is in.

Pleasure Without Sin

So how does this self-examination and cleanliness intersect with pleasure? The Bible says in Hebrews 11:24–25, *"By faith Moses, when he had grown up, refused to be called the son of Pharaoh's daughter, choosing rather to endure ill-treatment with the people of God than to enjoy the temporary pleasures of sin."* My point is that sin is pleasurable, but obviously all pleasure is not sin. As a matter of fact, more pleasure is available for the Christian than what is available for those who are not. God's provisional list is eternal.

So what is the root of pleasure? I will tell you what it is not: it is not the physical act itself. For example, I have friends who think Colorado snow skiing is the greatest thing since sliced bread. They cannot think of anything else more beautiful, exhilarating, and pleasurable. But I also have friends that could live a lifetime without ever seeing snow and would rather spend the day on the beach fishing, sunning, or surfing. Evidently, the enjoyment is found in what has been created inside the individual.

Sure we do things with our bodies, but we are always feeding the heart. Our heart is where Christ resides. One of the greatest truths I have learned about Christ is that my life is His life. Colossians 3:4 says, *"When Christ, who is our life, is revealed, then you also will be revealed with Him in glory."* Did you get that? My life, your life, belongs to Christ. This is His life. How exciting it was when I discovered that each day, I could transfer the care and concern of my life over to Christ. What a monumental stress relief.

Here is a worthy example: at my last church, the front office door was locked for security reasons. The office staff of 3–7 people is behind locked doors, yet people visit the office constantly throughout the day. When you arrive, there is a buzzer and camera on the left side of the door. A simple push of the button and one of the wonderful secretarial staff ladies buzzes you into the office. They take a glance at who is requesting entrance, and they allow the person to come in.

The same principle applies with God. If you transfer the care and concern of your life over to Him, then whatever comes your way, He has allowed it to be "buzzed" in. Christians love to quote "His ways are above our ways," but we so often stand in judgment of His ways. When God buzzes something through the door, we must put our feet to our faith. We must respond in faith. We must believe even when belief seems impossible.

I am the first to admit that each day, the news shares a story of some illogical, irrational, and heart-stopping tragedy. God's ways are truly above mine, as His pay grade is way above mine. But when I begin my day by transferring care, concern, and control over to Him, I am demonstrating that He is governing my life, not me.

My great friend Eric always tells me that transferring the concern of his life over to Christ on a daily basis "takes all the stress off." You want to dump anxiety and stress? Allow God to control your life. Maybe you should stop right now and transfer the care, concern, and control of your life over to Christ.

Perhaps one of the greatest gifts God has given man is the ability to enjoy this life, but He never intended for man to live this life apart from Him. Thus, we are created to enjoy life based on Christ's life in us. Pleasure for the Christian is not relegated to church, choir, and potluck dinners. Rather, pleasure for the born-again believer is found in enjoying the life Christ is living out through you. (And yes, sometimes that means snow skiing and surfing.)

So now I enjoy life, but I enjoy it much differently. How about you? What drives your pursuit of pleasure? Are you looking for a "promised land" in the land of self-indulgence? It is not there; there is nothing but illusions and broken promises there. Remember, I am not against doing things for self. Men work hard and should be able to enjoy the fruit of their labor. But whatever you do, do it with Christ. If Christ should not be a part of your activity, purchase, or adventure, then stop. Learn to pump the brakes. Anything that moves you away from Christ is evil and not to be trusted. Anything that moves you toward Christ or something you would do with Christ is trustworthy. The flesh is weak, and the flesh is not redeemed. Paul states in Romans 7:18, *"For I know that good does not dwell in me, that is, in my flesh; for the willing is present in me, but the doing of the good is not."* However, Paul does not leave us with only bad news, for he reminds us in Galatians 5:16, *"But I say, walk by the Spirit, and you will not carry out the desire of the flesh."*

The Lord has been with me through every flesh battle. I have never faced a temptation, battle, or difficulty where I did not know His presence. I have repeated Colossians 3:2 to myself thousands of times: *"Set your minds on the things that are above, not on the things that are on earth."*

When dealing with a difficult customer, an employee issue, rude drivers, disagreeable people, a bad attitude—anything that is tempting my flesh to flex its muscles—I simply start repeating that verse in my head over and over again. I may be dealing with what is in front of me, but in my spirit, I am asking God to intervene. King David said in Psalm 16:8, *"I have set the Lord continually before me; Because He is at my right hand, I will not be shaken."*

David knew and practiced what I try to do each day, and that is looking at life through Christ. I keep Him out front, He is the lens by which I view life now. Please, remember and remind yourself daily that there is a spiritual battle going on over your life, whether it is to keep you from responding to the gospel, or to damage your walk with Christ, or stop your impact and witness for Him.

Stu Webber, in his great book, *Spirit Warrior,* reminds us as he quotes Bill McCartney, founder of Promise Keepers, "We all know we are in a war. Our problem is that we are not at war."[10]

"Stay intentional," my buddy Eric reminds me often. Each of us know Christians who have fallen, myself included. It happens when we redefine pleasure.

Proceed with Caution

I will close this section with this warning. Be careful of the slippery slope, that flirtation with the flesh's definition of pleasure. I have been on that slippery slope—the other side of the mountain. This is where a Christian has no business. Since I have been a believer, I have experienced and seen in so many men the desire to reformulate God's path to joy and pleasure.

It often looks like this: years go by with a seemingly permanent victory over a sin area. One can "feel" they have conquered the stronghold Satan once had in their life—but forget that feelings will get them in trouble. I experienced those feelings myself. Then the next thing you'd know, I was testing myself and rewarding myself with bad behavior for the good behavior I had enjoyed. How insane. I felt so thrilled with myself that I would reward myself with bad behavior. I thought that I could once again manage my behavior. My flesh could never keep my flesh in check—it never worked. Nope, things always got worse.

So here is the truth about slippery slopes. Satan controls that slope; he is the master at it. If you go down his "slippery slope," you will find the first forty yards or so fitted with the best steps a carpenter could build. The slippery side of his slope seems manageable. I have fallen for that illusion that I could traverse this side of the mountain with no consequences. You move forty yards or so down Satan's pleasure side of the mountain, and suddenly, the mountain becomes like a piece of glass, slick as ice. You are no longer Satan's prospect; you are now his customer.

I hope and pray that you'll redefine your definition of pleasure. Enjoy life; enjoy it to the fullest. I like the KJV version of Revelation 4:11: *"Thou art worthy, O Lord, to receive glory and honor and power: for thou hast created all things, and for thy pleasure they are and were created."* God found pleasure in you, that is why He created you. Live your life finding pleasure in Him. With Christ, you can enjoy life without "apple pie."

Reflection Questions:

1. How do you define pleasure?

2. How has your life as a Christian impacted your definition?

3. Are you tempted to drink from the old well? How can you resist that temptation?

4. What are five areas of struggle in your Christian walk? Find five verses that speak to that area. Write these verses on an index card, place them in your pocket, and read them throughout your day when trouble, frustration, or sin comes your way.

5. Are you aware of Christ's presence in your life? How could you increase your awareness of His presence?

6. What is attractive about the slippery slope side of the mountain?

7. How does Christ's presence keep you on God's side of the mountain?

5

WHERE THE PROMISED LAND IS NOT FOUND—POWER

About Power

Power was my "cherry pie"—my second favorite pie. Merriam Webster offers this as one of its definitions of power: "Possession of control, authority, or influence over others," or "ability to act or produce an effect."[11] My definition, however, read a bit more like this: "The ability to act within one's own sphere of influence to direct things, by any means, in the direction one desires to complete one's own objective." In other words, pretty much, "Get it my way."

That is how we operated in the drug world. Power and control in themselves became the currency by which we operated while the object of the influence was secondary. The drug of "power" is so addictive.

It sounds like I am splitting hairs, for what good is power if there is not an object to exercise it over? But the possession of the power was more exciting than the results it delivered. The two are closely connected, but having power and influence was number one.

Power and strength were essential to a safe drug operation. In a sense, we were simply modeling the mode of operation for the world system, as any evening spent viewing the nightly news reveals stories of power struggle after power struggle. Power has become so essential to the success of politicians, governments, big business, and countries that it is obtained by almost any means. The depravity to which folks stoop today to gain power rivals the best of our attitudes during the drug years.

Each day we see how power possessed and exercised is more relevant than the people who are overseen. It is not people who get elected today, but rather ideologies and platforms, and people exercise whatever means are necessary to gain power. Satan and his demons know who to prop up as they scream from the airways and mountain tops to "be strong." But as all of us have learned, half-truths will get you into trouble. "Be strong" might be the rally cry from Satan and today's lost world, but as a half-truth, it becomes a lie. The world has embraced the lie to be strong in self, to pull oneself up by the bootstraps, to rely on self-determination–all half-truths that discard God.

Here in God's word, we find the rest of the truth. God says

in Ephesians 6:10, *"Finally, be strong in the Lord and in the strength of His might."* (Revelation 4:11) The world places a period after the word "strong." However, it is the rest of the verse that defines power and strength and from whence it is found. As you read through this book, you will see how Christ's presence in my life is my strength.

It is natural to have been influenced by someone; the list is long for each of us. Our hearts and minds are filled with inspiring encouragement from parents, grandparents, coaches, and teachers. I hope and pray that each bit of advice was well intentioned, but words of wisdom need to find their foundation, as pointed out in Ephesians 6:10, *"in the Lord."*

Simply put, God should influence everything we do and speak. Perhaps you have been told to be strong. My dad loved to say that to me. "Stay strong, bud, and remember you are a Hardy." I never quite knew what that meant. But I know now it was a half-truth.

Made to Influence

So what about power and influence? God intended for His children to be light and salt in this world. Christians are to bring light into dark places and people should become thirsty when spending time with us. Scripture says that God created man "for His pleasure," (Revelation 4:11) but also to be influential. Man was to nurture and subdue all of creation, and to exercise great influence over all of it. God created us to have influence for Him. Just as Israel was to be an influence for God in all the world, the Christian Church is to be an influence today.

Yet the shout of Satan to all the world to be strong in self has left the world wanting and dying in sin. As my life grew in strength without Christ, the moral planks began to erode.

Of course, this is the same rot which has infested America. Influence exercised without morality is totally self-serving. Man was to lend his voice, talent, and availability to God. He has given gifts to each of His children, and we are to use them for His glory. But too often, we take what God has given us for the purpose of giving back to Him and use it for self-promotion. This is when influence becomes the work of evil.

Of course, there is nothing nefarious about exercising influence and power if the one executing it is merely the conduit of the power rather than the originator of power. Just as electricity flows from the power line to the house, to the electrical panel, out to a light switch and then to a light, man was created to be the light switch—merely a conduit of God's influence and power.

We see this in the business world. Anyone in business, sports, or leadership who manages others knows their influence is for the greater good of the organization, not for personal gain. Those that do it for the power trip are eventually exposed, discarded, and labeled as "the guy who let it get to his head."

Obviously one does not have to be a Christian to own and operate a business. But the principles of the Bible certainly provide the right foundation to build on. I like what Truett Cathy, founder of Chick-fil-A, said: "Sometimes people ask if they have to be a Christian to work at Chick-fil-A. I say, not at all, but we ask that you make your business decisions based on biblical principles. There seem to be no conflicts when we tell people of various faiths how important it is to stick to the Scriptures in business decisions. In the Scriptures we learn how to handle our businesses, how to give customers good service, and how to treat employees."[12]

Cathy states, on Chick-fil-A's career webpage, that the reason they were in business was, "To glorify God by being a faithful steward of all that is entrusted to us. To have a positive influence on all who come in contact with Chick-fil-A."[13] That business model certainly has worked.

Looking for Shortcuts

But man has always struggled with how to handle their influence. Like I said, "Get it my way," has been man's problem since the Garden of Eden. Satan wanted to be like God. He wanted the power God possessed. It did not work out too well for ole Satan, for God cast him out, and a third of his cronies with him. Satan could not execute influence and power in the way he determined he should be allowed, in the place he wanted to exercise it, so God cast him out of heaven. Then he went after God's finest creation.

Now let me state this: I am not a theologian. I have read Sproul, MacArthur, Augustine, Barth, and others trying to understand how and why Adam sinned. I know there had to be a testing place for man's fidelity, and these modern-day theologians do a good job of explaining. But at the end of the day, I find myself still scratching my head. So let me propose a simple, where-the-rubber-meets-the-road explanation.

Adam and Eve were created without sin and with limited free will—but free will nevertheless in the sense that they were able to make choices that God allowed. So at the end of the day, what tripped them up? Number one, Eve engaged in a conversation with Satan, and that never works out well (Genesis 3:1). Not even Christ conversed with the ole dragon, choosing only to quote scripture (Matthew 4:3-11). Secondly, Satan raised doubt. Ultimately Satan convinced Eve that God was not a "nice guy." God had the audacity to withhold something good from them and to keep them from being whom they had a right to be (Genesis 3:4-5).

Eve was deceived, but she allowed it on the premise she could be "like God." The "lust of the flesh, the lust of the eyes, and the pride of life" manifested themselves in the pursuit of power. They wanted to do things their own way. They wanted to run the show, run the garden differently. And ultimately, they wanted a shortcut to what God had intended for them.

Remember, the "lust of the eyes" is not so much about lusting after the bikini-clad lady on the beach or the new Ram 2500 on the showroom floor. Rather, it is allowing your eyes to look for a shortcut to what God has promised you. As a result of caving to the shortcut temptation, the first couple was duped (Eve was deceived, Adam willingly rebelled) in the garden by the father of lies.

Think about it. Adam was told to subdue all of creation and bring it under control (Genesis 1:28). The message was to bring the *creation* under control, not the *creator*. But the temptation to be absolutely in control of everything caused them to lose everything. Power sneaks up on us. I do not believe Adam and Eve said, "Hey, we need to be in charge here! Who does God think He is telling us what we can and cannot do?" Here is what I believe their thought was: "Why should we have to wait? We want it now." This thought has permeated man's mind since the garden.

Remember that any time you sin you are believing a lie. It is Satan's lie that you can achieve God's plan differently than what God has planned. I believe Adam and Eve merely acted out of a heart that had taken its focus off God. They acted as man acts when God is not involved. Satan told the couple they would be like God if they ate of the fruit. Satan knew that was an impossibility, but he knew sin and the rippling effect of it. In man's attempt to "be like God," he blew right past the "like" part and went straight to the "as God" part.

Man has been playing God ever since the garden of Eden.

Man has settled on his own devices, seeking to achieve through influence what only the power and presence of God in an individual can bring. The oldest lie "Ye shall be as gods," is still being told today, and mankind is no closer to refuting the lie than when Adam and Eve fell victim.

Using Your Influence

Perhaps we all know what it is like to influence others. To "throw your weight" around to get something done. The little league, book club, and HOA meetings are filled with folks who are power-driven. The business world and financial world are filled with them. Is there something wrong with using your influence in your sphere of operation? Certainly not, for there is nothing wrong with a person exercising their gift of leadership to get things accomplished for the greater good of the people and organization in which they are involved. The influence of a sports coach over young men and women can mold them for a lifetime. A teacher influences her students to excel when in the past they had not. A police officer influences someone to get involved in their own community. Jack Welch, the great CEO of G.E., influenced dozens of folks who became leaders of many fortune 500 companies. Dwight Bain, an extraordinary, world-renowned counselor and life coach in Orlando, spends 6–8 hours each day helping people and influencing them with Godly direction. The bottom line is that we all influence others. So it is not the influence that is the key, but rather where it is ultimately directed.

When I was in prison, I found out I was not alone in committing crimes with my father. I met many men who simply followed in their dad's footsteps by selling drugs, committing robberies, swindling, conning people, and other acts of depravity. Their fathers, uncles, cousins, and brothers were direct influences on their life, and it manifested itself in them breaking the law, harming others, and going to prison. Both groups have two things in common: they were influenced by someone, and they each had a choice. We get to choose how we influence people, and we have the choice whether to accept the influence of someone.

The problem with power is that it is so easily misused. Power can become a pursuit that feeds egos and pride rather than a tool used to focus on helping others. And anything self-focused for too long turns into pride. The pursuit of power replaces what the power is to produce. The focus becomes not the object you are influencing, but rather the influence that drives the pursuit.

As I have grown in Christ, especially after I started reading the scriptures, one thing has become very clear: God never gives one the gift of influence for themselves. The gift of influence is to glorify God in the administration of the gift. However, the pursuit becomes a "promised land" for some. If they are in control wielding their influence, life is great. But let them take a back seat and things begin to fall apart.

Misused power is all about being served and never about serving others. And power-hungry people do not make good waiters.

I think of some of the people I know who are "control freaks." The privilege of being in power, usually for the first time in their life, has created a narcissism that is apparent to everyone but themselves. And we all know a narcissist cannot imagine anyone, including God, having a different opinion, suggestion, or plan other than their own.

During the drug years, power was a drug. The ability to influence others was mighty, and as I said, it spent like a currency. Money was a tool in the power toolbox. It could get a lot of things done. As a matter of fact, I had just about decided that everyone we encountered had a price. That happens when you have cherry-picked the crowd you hang out with. I remember Dad telling me he found that the dilemma was not whether a person would do something, but rather what was it going to cost. That was true so many times.

There is nothing wrong with money—it is all in how one earns and spends it. God has blessed so many of His people with wealth so they could in turn could bless others so that He receives the glory. But a person who has money and loves power will use them both to his detriment. Read through Proverbs; the wealthiest and wisest man got his butt kicked by both money and power. Both together is like a double-edged sword that is hanging like Damocles' sword over his head.

Physical Power

The use of physical power is also a "promised land" for many. The bigger and tougher one is, the more power they have, and the more valuable they feel. We see this demonstrated in sports arenas, with military powers, and even on the playground.

Here is an example. I shared with you about my friend Ralph who sold us the kilos. In the beginning, I talked to Dad about safety and security. How was I to remain safe? How could I be protected? I carried a gun, Smith & Wesson 45, but I was not a gunfighter. I always had people with me, but you learn in life you are often outnumbered.

Anyway, when I was in Miami trading money for cocaine, my dad would be in Nashville. He almost never came to Miami; he never wanted to meet with people. He used his influence over me and others to do all that work. One day, early on, he told me he wanted to ride with me to pick up Ralph.

I'd come to pick him up after he flew into town and he stated, "I am riding with you today."

"Okay," I replied. But my gears were already turning. This was a first, and I wasn't sure how Ralph was going to respond.

Nevertheless, Dad was with me. I pulled into the Pollio Tropical restaurant parking lot, and Dad got out of the car and climbed in the back seat so Ralph could sit up front.

Ralph was a tad nervous when he got in the car, but I quickly explained who was in the back seat. The two of them spoke briefly. I was nervous, as I could tell that Ralph was nervous.

My dad said he wanted to introduce himself to Ralph and go on a scenic drive. *Scenic drive? What?* I thought to myself.

Dad directed my turns from the back seat, and we slowly worked our way over from 24th Street to 8th Street. At 8th Street, Dad said to take a right at the light, then another turn, followed by one last turn. I followed his instructions and found myself on a street lined with small attractive houses on a cul-de-sac. Kids were playing out in the street.

When we'd driven about three houses down the street, my dad spoke up again. "Ralph, do you know who lives there in the third house on the right?"

There was a long pause. I could sense Ralph's tension. After some time, he spoke.

"Yes. My mama and papa."

My mind was racing. *What the heck is going on?*

Dad had me complete the cul-de-sac turn and head back toward his drop off. Then he spoke to Ralph.

"If anything happens to my boy, something is going to happen in that house."

Ralph understood.

The irony of Dad's macho statement is that people who like power and misuse power always feel as if they can out-power the other guy, so I am not sure Ralph was intimidated. But he was surprised. He never said a word to me about that incident. We treated each other with respect, but he had gotten a message that day. I will say this though: I never felt threatened by Ralph, and only on one occasion did we have a problem with other people, and Ralph and his crew took care of that. And to this day—and I guess forever since Dad is gone—I still do not know how Dad knew about the house and Ralph's parents.

But let me tell you something, that was a power trip. It was like something straight out of the gangster movies. I remember feeling proud of who my dad was, thinking he was a real tough guy looking after his son. My goodness, sin causes delusion. I knew stories about my dad and his friends, and they could be mean people, all under the guise of flexing their power to get things their way.

My dad spent his last 22+ years in prison still wanting to be in control. His prison time was miserable for him. Sure, he helped a lot of guys. He helped teach guys how to read and write. And he taught math and accounting. He taught English to his Mexican friends. (Dad had majored in Spanish and could still do very well.) I received many letters from guys letting me know how Dad had helped them. But I know he never surrendered his heart to his situation. He was in a terrible place emotionally—everything he was forced to live out was contradicted by a heart that was always fighting back. He was focused on the half-truth, to be strong. Up until his last days, he was still giving orders and still trying to be tough. He never accepted the rest of the sentence.

Stay in Your Coffin

The stark difference between my father and me when it came to our time in prison was that he was convinced he did not deserve what he received, and that it was because of people snitching on him that he was in prison. I, on the other hand, knew that I had broken man's laws and transgressed against God. On that day I invited Christ into my life, I knew I had confessed that I was not in charge of my life anymore.

Looking back on that last moment with Ralph in the car, when he shared with me he had met Christ, he was telling me that he was not going to be in control of his life anymore. I did not understand how God could run a life or how He could direct my life, but I did know that the buck did not stop with me anymore. And you know what, I remind myself of that each morning. I would like to say that I surrendered control of my life once and have been off and running since, but that would be a lie. Nope, each morning is a surrender to Christ's control and influence over my life.

I have a secret formula that I have used over the years—especially the last ten years. Many times, during the day, when I'm faced with a struggle, temptation, ego, things not going my way, or a pride issue, I quietly say to myself over and over, "Lord, fill me with your presence, with your Spirit and help me to fall in line with your influence."

Now let me say this; I know I am filled with the Holy Spirit as a born-again believer. I was sealed with His Spirit (as described in Ephesians 1:13). But so often, when my pride and ego rear their loud presence, I find that I must surrender one moment at a time. I have used that phrase thousands of times, for I still lust for "cherry pie."

My wife, Judy, has a funny but serious phrase she uses with me when I get out of line. When I start pontificating about someone, something, or my opinion, she will say, "You need to get back in your coffin."

Romans 6 repeatedly speaks of the old man being dead. Well, dead men live in coffins. Thus, when my lust for power takes over, she sends me back to where the old man is supposed to reside. On the walls in my office are several sticky notes with these words: "Stay in your coffin." Perhaps you need to post these notes in your home as well.

So, each morning as part of my **prayer** time, I **give thanks** for the influence and direction of Christ and the Holy Spirit. I give thanks for the **gifts** that I have been **gifted** from **God.** I **give thanks** that I have been **allowed** to teach for several years and lead the Men's Ministry at our church. I **give thanks** for the numerous men God **brings** across my path. I **give thanks** that God has **allowed** a once totally self-absorbed, pleasure and power-driven pagan to be redeemed and that He uses me to influence people for **His kingdom.** Remember, every "Paul" (saved, redeemed, and changed) was once a "Saul" (zealous for everything but Christ).

Please note the key words from the previous sentences: **prayer, God, give thanks, gifted, allowed, brings, His kingdom.** Each word is a reflection on God's influence and power. People that connect their prayer life to their daily life influence people for Christ.

Here is a great example. I have a good friend who is top-notch. I have been his life group and men's Bible study teacher for over six years. I thought I knew about influence ... and then this happened. Mike (yep, same name as me) is a great father, husband, son, and friend. He has slowly been rising in the power company for which he works. A couple of years ago he was transferred to South Florida where he was placed in charge of operations. This was a training ground for him. It was hard on the family with the 3+ hour commute and long weeks away from family. During this time, his father, stepfather, and father-in-law were all dealing with cancer. His wife was at home with the two kids.

With his position, he could have come home, but my buddy

did not use his influence to get extra time off or take a long sabbatical. Nope, he started a prayer ministry for the folks he encountered at his workplace. He began to ask God to reveal to him those that needed prayer. I was blessed to partner with him. He would call, email, or text almost weekly sharing a prayer concern. He did not have a weekly prayer meeting or meet at a church. He simply met these folks right where they were. He had asked God for a prayer ministry, and suddenly people were seemingly randomly sharing their struggles in conversation with my buddy.

Another amazing observation is that over half the folks he talked to did not have a relationship with Christ and were non-believers. What happened was amazing. He began to see people healed, hearts and attitudes change, and most powerfully, he was allowed to participate in God's work. Each time my phone dinged or rang and I saw his name, my heart leaped with joyful anticipation of who we were going to pray for this week and how God had worked in our prayers. The beautiful thing was that the life that was changed the most drastically was his—all because he allowed God to influence others through the influence he had in the workplace.

Mike taught me about influence. Mike's power was in the Lord.

The Source of True Power

Some of the most influential people in scripture were tough, well-worn, rugged, battle-hardened, and rough, but they knew they were powerless. I think of Peter in Mark 14.

This tough guy Peter bragged that he would never turn his back on the Lord saying, *"Even if they all fall away, yet I will not!"* (verse 29b).

"And Jesus said to him, 'Truly I say unto you, that this very

night, before a rooster crows twice, you yourself will deny Me three times."' (verse 30).

But Peter insisted, "Even *if I have to die with You, I will not deny You."* (verse 31b).

I believe Peter meant every word he stated. He thought he was tough and powerful, but he caved in. You probably know the story.

However, Luke lets us know that Jesus said in Luke 22:31–32a, *"Simon, Simon, behold, Satan has demanded to sift you men like wheat, but I have prayed for you that your faith will not fail ... "*

Peter would spend the rest of his ministry knowing that his strength was found only in the Lord. Peter, relying in his own strength, denied Christ, yet resting in the power of the Lord he preaches one of the most powerful sermons, amid a Christ-hating crowd, in Acts 2:14–30.

We see in Joshua 1, before Joshua led the Jewish people into the promised land, that God tells him three times, *"Be strong and courageous,"* (verse 9). God repeats that phrase in verses six, seven, and nine, and then finally relays how this will be possible at the end of verse 9: *" ... for the Lord your God is with you wherever you go."* This leader of Israel and a growing army of ragtag soldiers would learn that strength begins and ends with the Lord. He was a tough, strong man, but his strength was in the Lord.

I like the story in 1 Chronicles 28 where King David is encouraging his son, Solomon, to build the temple. At first David's words in verse 10 seem like a half-truth: *"Consider now, for the Lord has chosen you to build a house for the sanctuary; be courageous and act."* That's the advice the world gives; be strong, be brave, but just do it. However, David is not going to leave his son helpless and hopeless. He continues his speech in verse 20. *"Then David said to his son Solomon,*

'Be strong and courageous, and act; do not fear nor be dismayed, for the Lord God, my God, is with you. He will not fail you nor forsake you until all the work for the service of the house of the Lord is finished.'"

If these three men found their power and strength not in self, but in the Lord, what could I possibly hope to do in my own strength? As life has continued, I have learned to find strength in Christ. It has been a learning process, oftentimes by trial and error. I try to do it on my own and an error message pops up in my heart. As I have experienced the Lord's sustaining strength and presence over the years, it has emboldened me to trust more quickly and deeply. The encouragement has come in looking back. Never once have I not known the Lord's presence in my heart. And though at times I did not know what was happening or the direction a situation would turn, I did know I was not alone.

Never Alone

My friend Ben told me that during the Vietnam War, while in combat, he always felt much more secure when someone was with him in the foxhole. Just having that presence there made a huge difference. That is how my Christian walk has been. When I have been at my worst and weakest, I still have known the presence of Christ. By the way, my buddy Ben— he has Christ in his foxhole now.

Christ's presence has given me the power to always continue. So power and influence exist, but remember that they are gifts from God. No matter where you are, where you work, or what your title is, you have been allowed that place by God.

So, how are you handling your "power" or your "sphere of influence"? Whatever you may do, whether you're the

CEO of a Fortune 500 company, a mechanic, a stay-at-home mom, a salesman, or the clerk at a local big box store, how are you using your "power"? Do not shrink back from the position where God has placed you. Your position has been ordained by God. You are God's missionary disguised as an employee, boss, or owner. Remember my buddy. This is not about changing jobs or moving from CEO to an hourly position. This is not about giving up a position in your career or life, but rather shifting positions in your heart. This is about recognizing the source of real influential power in your life. And God's influence creates results that last for an eternity.

Is your influence going to be recorded as selfish or as "service and surrender" to Christ? Remember, if you are blessed to build wealth here on this planet, make sure it still pales in comparison to the heavenly treasure you are building. Earthly wealth stays here when we leave, but we can send heavenly wealth ahead. If you are blessed with a position of influence over one, ten, or one hundred people, make sure they know Christ is your power source.

Remember, God knows how to run your business and life better than you do. Remember this scripture: *"and what is the boundless greatness of His power toward us who believe. These are in accordance with the working of the strength of His might which He brought about in Christ, when He raised Him from the dead and seated Him at His right hand in the heavenly places,"* (Ephesians 1:19–20). Which power do you want working in you? Your power or the power that raised Christ from the dead?

Each day, Christ helps keep me off the "cherry pie" diet. He will do the same for you.

Reflection Questions

1. Has your name replaced God's in how you operate your life?

2. Are you shortcut-focused? Remember Adam and Eve; often a shortcut is believing Satan's lie.

3. Do you act deserving or are you giving thanks? Did you earn the gifts you possess or do you see them as gifted by God?

4. Are you running the show, or do you enjoy the position in which you find God has placed you?

5. Is it you who brings people into your sphere of influence, or do you look for the ones God brings your way?

6

WHERE THE PROMISED LAND IS
NOT FOUND—POSSESSIONS

About Possessions

My favorite time of year is Thanksgiving through the
Christmas season. All of the focus on family being together
and the incredible food trumps any other time of the year.
All calorie-counting vanishes for about 45 days. Turkey,
dressing, and mashed potatoes are wonderful, but Judy's

homemade pumpkin pie is the most anticipated treat each holiday season.

The lust for possessions was my "pumpkin pie." It is not lost to me that the pie of possessions corresponds with the gift-giving and receiving time of year. Obtaining things was my focus. I did not mind spending money on others, but I always made sure I was going to get what I desired. In addition, I held onto everything I acquired with an iron grip.

Money & Blindness

Money was a big issue for me. How do I get it? How do I spend it? How do I get more of it? I knew that work was the "how to get it" part, but what do you do when work does not provide adequately for the "spending it" part?

Well, most sane people wait and work until they can spend what is necessary. But I practiced insanity much of my years.

I am not sure where I picked up the lust for things. Bigger and better seemed to be the desire of my heart for as long as I could remember. My dad lived with the same desire. He had grown up poor, living just a few houses away from the trash dump. Grandma struggled to provide, and eventually other families took on my dad's two oldest brothers.

Dad and his brothers overcame their early obstacles in life through success on the football field. But athletics does not fill a heart permanently. Each of the brothers found wonderful success in their careers. However, it did not end well for any of them, as I can see now that their hearts were never full and satisfied.

After the drug bust, my grandfather who was my dad's stepfather but the man who raised him—and my aunt both told me basically the same thing regarding my father. They both indicated that Dad was still trying to get away from the "trash dump." Never mind the fact that he had become fabulously successful, some years earning a seven-figure income, and owned lots of toys. Though his address had changed, his heart was still in a barren place.

Then along I came, a true follower of my earthly father. First, I must say, I learned many wonderful things from my father, and have great memories of him. For many years, life was not bad with Dad. But, looking back, I know there was an undercurrent of emptiness that plagued his soul. He always seemed to be looking for the next big deal, never satisfied for too long. It's amazing what we learn through osmosis—both positive and negative.

We all practice behaviors and habits we learned from parents. How many times have you been told you are just like your mother or father? Each of us also knows the downside of caught behaviors that certainly never would have been taught to us. If something is in front of you long enough, you will begin to stare at it, and staring at it eventually creates involvement. The old saying is true: "If you sit in the barber shop long enough, you will eventually get your haircut." It just happens.

Osmosis is a covert operation, as both parties are seemingly blind to the process. It happens in the most natural setting and fashion. And, just as I experienced, most people fail to see that the acorn has not fallen far from the tree. When we are shaped unknowingly by events or people, we can develop a behavior or thought process that is seemingly justified, but is really a cancer slowly and quietly eating away at our heart. Folks like this are great at recognizing diseases in others while never recognizing their own affliction. Dad and I were both sick and spiritually blind.

Jesus commented on what happens when two spiritually blind folks get together, saying, *"A person who is blind cannot guide* another *who is blind, can he? Will they not both fall into a pit?"* (Luke 6:39b). So many folks live their life disease-ridden and blind. They seem to be living satisfied lives, but really, they are sick.

So often our lives are spent in bitterness and animosity towards folks who are not the problem. I discovered many years ago that if all my problems in life are relegated to things outside of myself, then I will always have problems. A simple mathematical observation reveals that the common denominator is *self.* I know too many Christians who are still laying all their problems at the feet of someone else—usually family.

It would be nice to blame all my mistakes on Dad, but that would be ridiculous and irresponsible.

During the reign of the Judges in the Old Testament, Israel is depicted as a continually disobedient child: getting in trouble, needing help, receiving help, and then starting the process over again. Samuel, the writer of Judges as mentioned by the Talmud, nails their problem in one verse: *"In those days there was no king in Israel; everyone did what was right in his own eyes,"* (Judges 21:25).

Those most afflicted by sin always share the common symptom of selfishness. In my case, I was simply practicing my own version of selfishness and greed. Over the years, many folks have spoken to me with anger at my father for leading his son into such depravity. Even my granddad told the prosecutor "You may not understand why Mike did what he did, but I do." He was referencing the influence of my dad.

But, as much as I understood Granddad's heart, he and the others were wrong. I made my own decisions. My heart was practicing what it knew best: selfishness and greed. A heart that is void of Christ is apt to any thoughts or behaviors; all bets are off for what behavior rises from an unregenerate heart. Where the rubber meets the road, I am responsible for my actions.

Defining Enough

How much is enough?

"Enough of what?" may be your first thought. But for now, let's define it this way: "enough" is the amount needed to fill your heart and soul permanently.

Just now, I typed that sentence into a Google search, and over five billion references were available. In the search for an answer to how much is enough, there is not enough time to search all the answers. So how do we know?

There is an answer; God has made sure of that. If you spend time reading the Bible, you will find a reflection of your heart—both pretty pictures and ugly pictures. Early in my Christian walk I discovered a great reflection on the ugliness of my heart. In reading the book of Haggai, I began to understand why I felt so empty in the wrong Promised Land.

In the story, the Jews have returned from Babylon, being released from captivity by a decree from Cyrus, the Persian. They find the city in ruins and the temple is decimated. So the people get busy fixing up their own stuff—while ignoring God's house. Their focus was on building wealth for themselves. And, well, maybe they would get to God's house once their own stuff was in good shape.

So Haggai speaks for God saying, *"You have sown much, only to harvest little; you eat, but there is not enough to be satisfied; you drink, but there is not enough to become drunk; you put on clothing, but there is not enough for anyone to get warm; and the one who earns, earns wages to put into a money bag full of holes.' The Lord of armies says this: 'consider your ways!'"* (Haggai 1:6-7).

Three different times the Lord says there is not enough. That was where I was. There just did not seem to be *enough*. Now, granted, I had no relationship with God, but nevertheless, I was looking for the "lust of the eyes", which is the devil's shortcut. As you will see, neither my dad nor I wanted to wait any longer. We needed a shortcut.

Shortcuts

In the years before the cocaine trade began, I made a decent salary. I had health insurance, investments set up for retirement, a home, two cars, a boat, and the promise of a continued career, as one day I would fill my father's shoes in his company. At least, that was the plan Dad and I often discussed. On top of my salary, our business was set up to pay out a bonus every four weeks.

I also had a wife and a son. My daughter would be born after the cocaine business began. Much like most families, we had our struggles: we were newlyweds, and raising children comes with a learning curve. But we were in good shape—at least, the best shape that man can provide. In spite of this, there seemed to always be a problem: the problem of having a diet the budget could not meet.

It seems that Dad had the same issue. He had mentioned several different ideas for increasing income. In 1994, we tried our hands at selling frozen seafood. Nothing seemed to produce the money we were looking for. Finally, the answer came, and empty hearts were ready to pounce.

My dad and I were sitting at table #10 in our restaurant—a round table with room for eight in the back corner. Pictures of Ernest Hemingway's house and scenes of the ocean hung from the walls surrounding us. A friend of mine and his father were in the restaurant too, and Dad asked them to join us. I was quietly grateful, because I was tired of hearing the "We are not making the money I thought we would," speech.

My buddy was a real character, having served eight years in prison, and he was no stranger to the drug world. His dad, who had retired long ago, also had been quite a character in his day. Dad and I really liked these guys. They were authentic, what-you-see-is-what-you-get type men. They made no excuses for their past or their present behaviors. You never knew what direction a conversation with them would take.

At the invitation, they joined us at our table. We waved a waitress over to take our order and get us some drinks. My dad almost always drank water, but on this day, he ordered unsweetened tea. He said he'd wanted to taste the flavor of the unsweet tea, but one sip convinced him otherwise.

"It tastes good for unsweet tea, but it needs some sugar," he said.

My buddy reached over to the table caddy filled with condiments, grabbing for the sugar dispenser. But as he went to pass it along to Dad, the lid came off, and the dispenser flipped over, dumping all of the sugar out on the table. Using his hand to scrape up the mess, my buddy said, "Man, I could put this in a bag and sell this."

His dad nodded. "Plenty of money in that sugar."

My dad's eyes lit up, suddenly very interested. "Is that right?"

"Are you kidding?" my buddy said. "The cost is so cheap, it can be sold anywhere north of Florida for big money."

I immediately tensed up, feeling very uneasy about the turn of the conversation. I had struggled with a cocaine addiction for a few years and was nervous to even hear the word cocaine around my dad. I knew he was not ignorant of the drug or the selling of it—I knew stories of some folks he knew back in Nashville. But he had been upset about those people and their situations. There at that table, I did not want to endure another conversation revisiting my addiction years. Thankfully, the conversation moved on. But a seed had been planted—an evil seed.

The growth of a cotton seed is a good analogy for what happened next. Upon planting a cotton seed 2 1/2 inches below the soil, with the right temperature and soil conditions, it will immediately begin to grow downward. The taproot can grow up to ten inches downward, and after 7–10 days, the first cotyledons break through the surface. An identical process takes place in the human mind and heart. Things grow in our hearts and minds long before the thought is manifested. As my Christian brother Dave always says, "Thoughts become actions."

This same truth shows up in scripture. James 1:14–15 says, *"But each one is tempted when he is carried away and enticed by his own lust. Then when lust has conceived, it gives birth to sin; and sin, when it has run its course, brings forth death."*

That conversation over the table sugar produced a seed that would reap a huge harvest—a harvest of destruction. Seeds always produce a harvest of what was planted, in a greater number than what was planted, and much later than when it was first planted. As I stated earlier—short-term gain produces long-term pain.

Short-Term Gain

As I mentioned in the first chapter, $40,000 was spent on my first day's kilo purchase. But by 1996, that number was in the seven digits. The profits were huge. Dad and his partner were making nearly $500,000 on each transaction. I was being paid well too but elected to mostly allow my father to hold my money. Not wanting to miss out on all the spoils of our work, I did keep plenty of cash in my closet safe. But it wasn't near the cash dad was holding.

I used the money I took home to finance a life of ease. It bought a new house, boats, vehicles, trips, and plenty of extravagance. Rented Lear jets and limos were a couple of favorite expenditures. There was nothing that was unobtainable; it seemed that money could buy everything I desired. Of course, that can only happen when one's desires are relegated solely to feeding the flesh.

I was generous with the money as well. Plenty of folks benefited from our generosity. The profits of the cocaine business had grown exponentially, oftentimes doubling each month. It grew so fast; it seemed like a blur. We were blinded, I was blinded by the money and its provisions.

In the end, I was charged with money laundering in a drug conspiracy, laundering tens of millions of dollars. Looking back, not one dollar we made or spent produced one ounce of integrity, character, or morality. Money is a poor substitute for those things. It never provided a fulfilled heart. I had all that money, and yet there I had a sense of emptiness. That emptiness produced a desire to seek more, but as I discovered, a focus on money and things will only produce a greater, more intense focus on money and things. Thus, money and its purchasing power had me in its grip. But thanks be to God, He would rescue me from this feigned Promised Land.

The Diagnosis

It was on that September day in 1997 that God placed a thermometer in me. A disease detector. It has been my walk with the Lord that has led me to discover my "diseases," whether self-inflicted or received through assimilation unknowingly. God has been faithful in revealing them in me, as His Spirit has been faithful to not leave me the way He found me. It has been His work in my heart that has removed sin as the controlling influence in my life and monitored my spiritual temperature. Of course, it is not His diagnosis alone that brings healing, but it is the beginning. It is the application of medicine that brings about restoration.

I keep this verse written on my desk or on my office wall: *"Search me, O God, and know my heart: try me, and know my thoughts: And see if* there be any *wicked way in me, and lead me in the way everlasting,"* (Psalm 139:23–24, KJV). It is in these words where I discovered the diagnosis, the medicine, and the healing.

Initially, it seemed that the weaning off of materialism would be easy, as I was going to be in prison. Surely time away from the luxuries of life would break anyone's focus on them. But nothing could be farther from the truth. Sadly, many men in prison spend their time fantasizing, preparing, and sharpening their old skills.

Upon my arrival in prison, I began a faithful prayer life and started reading through the scriptures. As I read, I always had one book of the Bible on which I was focused, while at the same time reading the scriptures from beginning to end. One thing became increasingly clear as the stories of God's people became more and more alive to me: God is focused on our heart.

I discovered that it was not the poverty of possessions that conflicted me. Sure, everything might have been physically taken away, but my heart and mind still held closely to things. It was the prospect of the poverty of my soul that I had begun to wrestle with.

The possession of pride and selfishness had an unyielding grip on me. Up until then, I had been self-sufficient, proving by whatever means necessary that I could take care of myself.

As I read through the book of Genesis, I became fascinated by the stories of Abraham, Jacob, and Joseph. It was the story of Jacob in particular that spoke to my heart, broke my heart, comforted my heart, and changed my heart. I found that I could align the template of Jacob's life directly with mine (aside from having twelve sons that brought about the nation of Israel, of course).

I encourage you to take a look for yourself. See if you can see your own life in Jacob's story as well.

Wrestling with God

Jacob was born second, perhaps only minutes after his twin brother, Esau. Rebekah, their mother, knew she was having twins, and she knew they would be at odds with each other. The Lord spoke in Genesis 25:23, *"'Two nations are in your womb; And two peoples will be separated from your body; And one people will be stronger than the other; And the older will serve the younger.'"*

The name Jacob meant *supplanter* or *deceiver.* Right off the bat, that defined who I was. I had lived a life of deception— mostly self-deception. Of course, we know that God's sovereignty was at work, for He had said, *"the older would serve the younger,"* but Jacob was still a conniving individual. In the story, we see that he steals twice from Esau: first his birthright, then the blessing from their father, Isaac.

Jacob traded Esau a bowl of beans for his birthright. I initially thought Esau was an idiot. But self-inspection and a glance backwards revealed I had traded away much for what amounted to "bowls of beans."

After taking everything from his brother, Jacob left home running from Esau. His brother wanted to kill him. It is here that scripture records the events of one of the first desert nights under the stars. There, Jacob has a dream; we tell the story today referring to it as Jacob's ladder. Genesis 28:12 states, *"And he had a dream, and behold, a ladder was set up on the earth with its top reaching to heaven; and behold, the angels of God were ascending and descending on it."* What is so beautiful is that the words "on it" can also be translated "on Him." Jacob saw our Lord.

In his dream, the Lord spoke saying, *"'Behold, I am with you and will keep you wherever you go, and will bring you back to this land; for I will not leave you until I have done what I have promised you,'"* (Genesis 28:15). What comfort. What an incredible God we serve. Those were my first thoughts after reading this. I found comfort in knowing that Christ was present and working in a selfish guy like Jacob. Surely He would also work in my life.

With God as his sovereign guide, Jacob continued his journey. He met a man named Laban, and for twenty years he labored under him to earn the privilege of marrying his daughter. (I am fast-tracking this story a bit, but you can go back and read the story of Jacob's life in Genesis 25–35.) After twenty years, Jacob finds the right moment and flees from Laban taking Rachel and Leah with him. Laban pursues and after seven days he catches up with Jacob and his large caravan. There is tension initially, but God intervenes, and Laban makes a covenant with Jacob. Jacob continues as he is set to reunite with his brother, whom he had betrayed. He was about to reach his rock-bottom.

Dr. Bryan, my prison counselor, defined rock bottom as "the place where one turns around and never goes back." I think that's a perfect explanation and definition.

On Jacob's way home, a beautiful confrontation takes place. Scripture reports that he was alone, and along came a man who wrestled with Jacob (Genesis 32:24). The wrestling match would last until the early morning hours. Hosea 12:3-5 tells us that the man was the angel of the Lord, which is the pre-incarnate Christ.

I, too, have wrestled with God. This is where I am knit with Jacob. Jacob was tough; he was not going to give in or give up. His self-sufficiency kept him wrestling. He was determined to fight to hold onto "self." "I don't need to change," and, "So let's quit wrestling God," is the cry of the proud, unregenerate heart. How would this fight end? Well, here is what I have learned about wrestling with God: He sets the time limit on the fight. He knows what we need and what it takes to get us to the place where our dependence is on His provisions.

As the fight wore on, Jacob knew he could not prevail. Scripture says that his thigh had been thrown out of joint; he was now limping. But Jacob needed to leave the fight with something. So he asked the man for a blessing.

The man asked him his name, and he replied, "Jacob." Jacob, the name meaning supplanter and deceiver, was how he referred to himself. But that is the "old man." And here is the truth: the old man cannot enter the Promised Land. The man Jacob could not enter the promised land.

So God changed his name to Israel. A new man, a regenerated heart that would enter the land. In that wrestling match, Jacob discovered the poverty of his spirit. From that moment on, Jacob knew that self-sufficiency would never suffice. No longer would Jacob trust in himself; he now needed God. After this encounter, Jacob walked differently physically and spiritually.

I find it interesting that Jacob then asked for the man's name. I must believe he already knew. I have had many wrestling matches in my soul; I no longer have to wonder who I am wrestling with. Just as He wrestled with Jacob, God dealt with my inner man (and still does to this day) in the same way.

Perhaps, you have also been a Jacob. Maybe it is time for a name change. You will not need to change the name on your driver's license, but you will change your perception of yourself. You'll begin to see yourself as God sees you.

Losing my Grip

Since coming to Christ, the Promised Land has changed, and my grip has loosened. I now try not to grip anything, but merely balance it in my hands. I enjoy whatsoever the Lord has provided, reminding myself that I am the steward and not the owner. Things and money only belong to us for a season at best. Everything we own will belong to someone else someday. When we keep a tight grip on what belongs to God, we set ourselves up for pain, as it seems to always hurt when God removes something from our hands.

We have to trust that God never takes from us what we need. It took me some time to learn this lesson. God, in His wisdom, knew what it would take to break me. It began with understanding ownership. Looking back, I now know that I could not point to one thing I owned and say, "God provided that." Nope, my name was etched on everything I owned. There was not one purchase that had touched my soul.

The words of the wealthiest and wisest man ever to live ring so true in my ears and heart. Solomon had grown old, and he had wealth beyond measure—so much that silver was as stones on the city streets, he had wives by the hundreds, he had 10,000 horse stables. But at the end, when looking back at his life, he said, *"Vanity of vanities, saith the Preacher, vanity of vanities; all is vanity,"* (Ecclesiastes 1:2, KJV). Solomon spent some time in the Promised Land of possessions and he found out what I discovered: none of his stuff touched his soul or his heart with permanency. Scripture is not clear on what brought about his change of heart, but we can be certain God was working on him.

Walking in the Valley

After September 6th, I waited and hoped for the "easy button" to arrive, but it never did. Neither has it in your life. Even with Christ in my life, life as I knew it unraveled. Wealth vaporized and possessions dwindled. Initially, I struggled with God as I watched things go away. Yet, though the struggle was real, I invariably knew His presence. It's crazy; I had so much concern and worry for my family as my wealth began to disappear, but I did not have that concern when smuggling cocaine. Why? Greed is the answer, and all greed is the result of pride.

The husband, as my friend David P says, is to be the provider, protector, and the priest; I had been the bank. I thought money made a family happy. Money may provide for things, but it does not provide integrity, fidelity, love, and faith. It did not take long for this bank to collapse.

When I went to prison, we had only $500 in the bank. Everything was gone, including our life insurance, retirement, and investments. So as I watched the Lord take care of my family while I was away, He took me through the wilderness. Many times I felt as if I was in the valley of despair. But with Christ, I have learned to not fear the valley. Traverse this great nation from coast to coast, and you will find fertile soil in the valley; things like to grow there.

Thus it was in the valley where the fertile soil of faith began to produce fruit. It was in the valley where God would break me and teach me to trust Him. What at first seemed to be a lonely place became the place of total abundance. Remember, the Jewish people also walked in the barren land for forty years before entering the Promised Land. Here is the work of God in the valley: He takes you to a seemingly empty place and strips you barren. But with the presence and promise of our Lord, one finds he is not alone in the valley.

Psalm 23:4–5a reveals the abundance and presence of God in the valley: *"Even though I walk through the valley of the shadow of death, I fear no evil, for You are with me; Your rod and Your staff, they comfort me. You prepare a table before me in the presence of my enemies."*

Our Lord guarantees two things. Number one: you are going to be in the presence of tough times. David makes this clear in his psalm with the statements "I fear no evil," and "the presence of my enemies." Evil must have been close. However, here is the second guarantee: God says he gave us a table in the valley, in the face of the evil we will encounter. That evil manifests in areas like doubt, failure, guilt, sin, temptation, loneliness, sorrow ... simply everything that Christ took to the cross.

What is on that table? I have found it to be a buffet table filled with His presence and provisions. Every spiritual provision needed to traverse the valley is spread about the table. Christ said of Himself *"'I am the bread of life; the one who comes to Me will not be hungry, and the one who believes in Me will never be thirsty,'"* (John 6:35b).

What is this bread we partake of? It is the word of God. In the valley, I found that feasting on the word of God kept me aware of Christ's presence, and without fail gave me the weaponry to battle that which was in front of me. (Remember those five index cards?) The spiritual body cannot live without spiritual food any more than the physical body can live without physical food. Additionally, it would be foolish to think that the spiritual could touch the physical need, or the physical to touch the spiritual need. So it was in the valley where I learned the futility of my possessions and money.

It was in prison where I first encountered this verse found in 1 Timothy 6:7: *"For we have brought nothing into the world, so we cannot take anything out of it, either."* I had heard that saying before but had no idea it came from the scriptures. Our Lord would teach me that the time between "brought nothing" and "cannot take anything" is to be filled with our faithful stewardship of His provisions. I had not a clue as to what I would encounter in the valley or in the Promised Land. But one thing I did know: the fullness of Christ and His promises would see me through. Just as Christ worked in my life, I hope and pray that with His presence you will transform your lust for possessions—that "pumpkin pie"—and exit the valley closer to Christ than when you entered.

First Temptation and Victory

After the initial drug bust on August 15, 1997, my dad went on the run for about eight days. Most of our crew was sitting in jail in Nashville. Even the pilot who had flown one of our partners with that last load of kilos to Nashville was in jail with a huge bond. Here is the crazy part about our pilot: he was innocent. Never one time did me or dad ever discuss with him or tell him what we were doing. Dad used to tell me "If you ever tell someone what we are doing it will cost ten times what we are paying now." So we never told him.

After several days on the run, Dad finally turned himself in and posted a million-dollar bond. Meanwhile, I sat nervously in Key West, waiting for the feds to arrive. Dad was in and out of jail a few times—he would get arrested again on new charges, post bail, and then be out again. By late September, things were really starting to unravel. The loyalty that Dad had counted on from his partners was eroding, as each person was focused only on self-preservation. All his macho talk that "No one will speak, they know what will happen," became just a vapor in the wind. Everyone was talking. The chips were starting to fall, and eventually nearly thirty people came under indictment.

By this time, I had hired two attorneys and was waiting for the knock on my door.

"Hey bud, I need you to meet me in Atlanta, the Marriott at 285 & 75. Can you be there in two or three days?" Dad said over the phone.

"No problem," I said. "But what is this about?"

"We need to talk," he replied.

I had been hoping for this, as we had not communicated much since his arrests. I did not know what to think, what to do, what was going to happen. What was his story? What was my story supposed to be? What about my family? What about my safety? I didn't know much but I did know this: I had invited Christ into my life on September 6th, and I was constantly aware of something inside me.

I drove to Atlanta, where we met and talked. He was focused on trying to tell me the "story" we were supposed to tell the feds, so we could both be on the same page. He wanted us to rehearse the story together. It was pitiful and made as much sense as Grape Nuts cereal—which has neither grape nor nuts.

I told my dad, "Dad, my attorney says, 'Do not be the last man in the boat, you have to look out for yourself.'"

He replied, "I will be fine, I may get sentenced to 10 years and hopefully be out in 6."

He eventually was sentenced to 35 years.

After rehearsing the story, he handed me a stack of paperwork.

"What is this?" I asked.

"This is information for some banking that I have done outside this country," was his reply. He motioned for me to sign.

The next few seconds felt like minutes as my mind raced from my profession of Christ to my talk with Len to my attorneys. I had stated to all of them—Christ, Len, and the attorneys—that I was walking away from the drugs and money.

So, with strength I had not previously owned, I told my dad, "Dad, I'm not signing anything. I do not want anything, and I do not want to know anything."

I am not sure how I kept my promise to Christ, other than something inside of me that told me to say no. Some might say it was fear of getting into more trouble—I do not know, but I know at that moment my heart pushed back.

Dad was upset. He could not understand. He reminded me of the money he was holding for me and that one day my family would need it.

"I am not interested," I told him.

Here is a bit of information that is so ironic about my money situation on the day of the bust. After that day with Ralph in May 1997, I was bringing in very little money from the business, as I was basically not working. Since Dad was keeping my money for me, my closet safe funds were shrinking. On that day in May 1997, instead of having upwards of hundreds of thousands of dollars, I maybe had $4000 in my home safe. On September 7, 1997, I gave $2000 of that money away to a family that needed help, and I kept $2000. I never again took a penny from the drug money. Solomon said, *"Do not weary yourself to gain wealth; Stop dwelling* on it. *When you set your eyes on it, it is gone. For* wealth *certainly makes itself wings Like an eagle that flies* toward *the heavens,"* (Proverbs 23:4–5). That certainly applies to ill-gotten wealth.

I want to share with you a verse that stopped me in my tracks; I literally sat motionless and speechless for what seemed like an hour when I first read it. Jeremiah the prophet wrote, *"As a partridge that hatches eggs which it has not laid, So is a person who makes a fortune, but unjustly; In the middle of his days it will abandon him, And in the end he will be a fool."* (Jeremiah 17:11). Wow. There it was—the script for my life. God's word is such a powerful teacher. It is the best teacher; it trumps experience every time.

Lessons in the Valley—Short-Term Pain

Over the past year, I have been involved with several folks as they entered rehab. I help in every step of the process I can: searching out the information, driving them to the facility, and sticking around until they finally walk through the doors to their housing for the next 3–6 months. Not one time has anyone been allowed to bring any of their old paraphernalia with them. Absolutely nothing that connected them to that devastating world they were trying to leave was permitted in the facility. This was a place for implementing change.

My prayer was always the same: that they would exchange a new way of life for the old. Seems like a no-brainer, doesn't it? Well, the same principle applies with our Lord as we surrender our life to Him. He is not going to allow any of our worldly attitudes or things to rest in the Promised Land. Note that I used the word *rest*. Christians do struggle with old sin, temptations, and accoutrements of society, and we try to hold onto these things, but there is never a rest or a peace when trying to hold onto these things in God's Promised Land. The Promised Land is the place for those who have experienced an exchanged heart: the old, ugly heart traded away for the heart of Christ.

This promise is found in 2 Corinthians 5:17: *"Therefore if anyone is in Christ, this person is a new creation; the old things passed away; behold, new things have come."* I had read that verse early in my Christian walk and I believed it. However, it was Christ who would teach me what a new heart was to look like. Thus the process of breaking me down would begin.

The nearly three years before I waited to go to prison was a time of learning and trusting. As my family watched the house, vehicles, boat, furniture, money, and other things go, the mounting weight of my actions was at times overwhelming. How would I be able to provide? Bottom line, I could not in any shape or fashion. Yet in those early months and years, God provided. Thanks be to God, a loving Church and a forgiving, loving family in Virginia Beach, my wife and children never went without. Though my ex-wife and I are no longer together, I remain forever grateful to her and her family.

I mentioned in the previous chapter about my first months in prison, but let me tell you about day one. I had finally arrived in Petersburg, VA some thirty days after being taken from court in handcuffs. I and thirty other prisoners, shackled hands and feet, had just arrived and been paraded into the prison and placed four to a cell.

Then orientation began. A guard, with a pin on his chest for twenty-four years of service, commenced with the reading of the rules. After this process, it was on to the laundry to get our clothes. I do not know what I was expecting, but it was not this. I received five pairs of green pants, five green button shirts, five pairs of socks, five pairs of underwear, five T-shirts, and one pair of steel-toed boots, all used. I will never forget what the guard tasked with handing out the clothing said to the group, "You guys must like wearing other people's underwear, because some of you I am seeing for the second time."

Two things jumped out at me: first of all, I was wearing used old underwear and t-shirts. But secondly, some of these guys were back for a round two. As I've said, I learned that it is not time that fixes problems, but what one does with the time that makes the difference. This is why the recidivism rate is so high in prison—the prison system is not equipped to help facilitate a changed heart, and most inmates are not working on the self.

I had left the courtroom in a new suit, and I was now in someone else's clothes.

Not long after, I was taken to my first cubicle. There wasn't much room. I had a locker, 36 inches by 18 inches. Everything I would own for the next few years would have to fit in that locker. On top of that, one realizes in prison that it is not really your locker, but rather it belongs to the prison, and a guard can open it whenever he desires. Additionally, everything in that locker belongs to the prison—even your personal letters, books, and such. Sure, they may belong to you, and you may leave with them one day, but everything you receive is subject to be read by someone else. There is no privacy. Many times in the first month, I thought of the house where I had lived, the privacy of a bathroom, the space of the back yard, and the importance of freedom. I can tell you, there were lots of soul-searching moments.

It was an attention-grabbing experience. To be honest, I wanted to have a pity party, but the promises of scripture prevailed. The three years before being sentenced provided time for much Bible study and limited application. I was now in the place where application was needed daily. In the end, if we are just reading the truth and not applying it, we are just building up head knowledge.

I had decided upon my arrival at prison that my first private Bible studies would center around the prison epistles. It was fascinating that God had taken a guy named Saul, changed him to a guy named Paul, and that guy, who had persecuted Christians and mocked our Lord, wrote 13 books of the New Testament—and four of the letters were written from prison.

So there I was, reading Paul's letters, and these two familiar promises jumped out at me: *"And my God will supply all your needs according to His riches in glory in Christ Jesus,"* (Philippians 4:19). And then, *"I can do all things through Him who strengthens me."* (Philippians 4:13).

I remember reading those verses and making the decision that I was going to trust in the truth of those promises. Here is what God revealed to me. Number one, He was providing for me. I had everything a man would need. I had clothes, shoes, food, water, a bed, and my Bible. My needs were perfectly being met. Number two, I learned the meaning of His strength. This began with learning what it is not. It is not the strength that I call on to do something physical—the strength to run a certain speed in the 40, squat a new personal record, or finish a task. Though His presence often has been the encouragement for athletes, students, moms, and such, this is not what Paul is referring to in this verse. Paul states in verse 12, *"I know how to get along with little, and I also know how to live in prosperity; in any and every circumstance I have learned the secret of being filled and going hungry, both of having abundance and suffering need."*

The strength Paul received from Christ was the ability to live in and under any circumstance. I read his words and tried to picture him in prison. I knew that those verses were promises to me, and sometime in mid-March 2001, I quit dreaming about how it used to be and got focused on what Christ was doing in my life in the present.

Psalm 23—Long-Term Gain

I had always had a comfortable home—maybe not a large home, but I wanted a comfortable home. My goal was that every piece of furniture could be somewhere where I could take a nap. Well I can tell you there are no Serta or Stearns and Fosters mattresses in prison. A metal frame and plate mimic a box-spring in most places, and pillows can be a rarity depending on where you are. But it is a bed, and I was thankful for each one that was provided. I'd made up my mind that I was not going to complain about God's provisions. The promises of the scriptures kept that commitment alive.

Perhaps the worst physical environment was in the Atlanta USP holdover unit. No frills of any sort. Two hours outside the cell each week and 2–3 showers a week, maybe. Anyway, it was prison—it was not supposed to be like the Marriott Courtyard. While I was there, I ended up in a cell by myself. I loved being alone. On day two, I bribed one of the orderlies (who bring our meals to us and pass them through a slot in the door) with three days of dessert to find and bring me a Bible. He found the Bible, about two thirds of one, and for three days, sure enough he took the dessert off my plate. No problem—I got the better end of the deal.

The days in a locked nine foot by eight foot room can get boring, especially when in that space for 48–72 hours. I developed a routine. I would place the Bible on the top bunk, open to an area I was reading, and walk back and forth from the bunk to the door, all nine feet, all day long. Each time I approached the bunk, I would read a verse.

It was this routine that allowed me the opportunity to memorize scripture. This is when I memorized the 23rd Psalm, where the words of that wonderful promise became so true in my heart and experience. I would walk from about

8 a.m. until 8 p.m., throwing in some push-ups along the way. It was in that study and meditation on the 23rd Psalm where I learned the truth about possessions and comfort. Let me remind you of those words (in the King James, because that is how I memorized it):

"The Lord is my shepherd; I shall not want. 2 He maketh me to lie down in green pastures: he leadeth me beside the still waters. 3 He restoreth my soul: he leadeth me in the paths of righteousness for his name's sake. 4 Yea, though I walk through the valley of the shadow of death, I will fear no evil: for thou art with me; thy rod and thy staff they comfort me. 5 Thou preparest a table before me in the presence of mine enemies: thou anointest my head with oil; my cup runneth over. 6 Surely goodness and mercy shall follow me all the days of my life: and I will dwell in the house of the Lord for ever."

I was learning, would learn, and am still learning, that the Shepherd takes care of His sheep's needs. The sheep is mostly a dumb animal and needs the shepherd to survive. The shepherd must guide the sheep into the green pastures, for he has no honing device that allows him to search out the grass. A sheep will starve to death seeking to eat dirt where the grass once was instead of moving to a new area.

In addition, a sheep does not have much of an internal GPS system, as a sheep can easily wander off and not find his way back to the flock. The shepherd must keep them close and within eyesight. God had me fenced in; I was not wandering off. Thus it was in that prison cell where I first knew that as a truth in my life. It was there that I learned the true definition of a "green pasture"; any place where I was alone with God was a "green pasture." It had nothing to do with the physical comfort of the place. I do not want the Waldorf Astoria presidential suite if God is not with me. Nope, give me the prison cell where He is located.

The last five days I spent in the prison cell were like heaven on earth. Nothing threw me off my focus, nothing plagued my heart. Though I missed my family and prayed for them, my heart was at complete peace. The more I was aware of His presence, the more I thanked Him for His presence, and the more alive the scriptures became. It was there that I first discovered the living Word, as the words seemed to leap off the page and blanket my heart and person.

God had prepared a table for me: it was Christ, and He the living Word of God (John 1:14) was laid out on the top bunk in a dirty prison cell. The buffet was laid out for me, the open Word of God, waiting for me to devour. The more I partook, the more I rejoiced. I had revival in that prison cell. The verse that speaks, "my cup runneth over," (Psalm 23:5) became a spiritual marker for my walk with Christ. Why? Well, for the Lord to run over in one's life, one must first be empty of self. There is no filling of the Holy Spirit, no filling of the Lord's presence, no understanding of the Word when one is filled to any degree with self. You may be eating in a green pasture, but soon you will be down to dirt. The indispensable truth is that the Lord works where there is an empty vessel. Oh, how thankful I am for that prison cell.

New Definition

The Lord continues to work in this area of my life. I have not taken a vow of poverty nor sworn off vacations, new clothes, vehicles, or anything else that the Lord allows us to enjoy. I just understand now that everything I do, everything I possess, and everything I purchase needs to have Christ as the foundation.

Judy and I try to live a life of thanks. She does a better job than I, but we are mindful that God is the provider and we are the stewards. We simply consider everything we have control over as belonging to our Lord. We practice the "somebody" method of sharing what God has given us. It is impossible to help everyone you meet that needs help. Of course a kind word, a listening ear, and the love of the gospel should be shared whenever possible. But the world is filled with hurting, needy folks who need real tangible help. Thus we always have a "somebody" that is the center of our hearts when it comes to sharing our time, attention, or money.

One of the best paths to keep the heart from loving your stuff too much is to give some of it away every now and then. Perhaps you have struggled with possessions. You have climbed to the mountaintop of self-appeasement and toy purchases, yet there seems to be something continually lacking. The heart just does not feel satisfied. Nothing you own has touched your soul. Or perhaps you have moved God out of the center and you are off balance. God promises He will take care of you. He knows all your needs, and He provides the strength you need for any circumstance. I hope and pray that today is the day that you switch from a pie-in-the-sky to His buffet table—all you need is there waiting on you.

Reflection Questions

1. What is your number one possession? (If you're unsure, what was it that popped into your mind initially?) What would your spouse and/or kids say your number one possession is?

2. Why have you placed such value on this possession? What does it provide?

3. Would you define yourself as a steward or an owner? How can you separate yourself from ownership?

4. Which behaviors are your children picking up from you through assimilation?

5. How full of self are you? Is there room for God to fill you with His presence?

6. What verses will you write on your index cards? Where will you keep them?

7. What is your definition of a "green pasture?"

7

WHERE THE PROMISED LAND
IS NOT FOUND—POSITION

About Position

Position—or having a title—was my "blueberry pie." But to be honest, I'm not a huge fan of blueberry pie on its own. I much prefer a "mixed berry pie." I especially love the flavor of blueberry and cherry combined. There's nothing like tasting those two mixed inside a glaze and filled with chunks of brown sugar cinnamon crisp. They work better together, for cherry pie—power—is best exercised from a position or title, and the higher the position, the more power.

Yet, though power and position go together, position on its own was a promised land for my heart. Nothing satisfied my lust for value and significance like having a title. Whether it was finally getting that position of "Football Team Captain," "Shift Leader," "3rd Relief Manager," "Assistant Manager," "Manager," and eventually, "Owner," it did not matter. I wanted to earn that title.

Obviously in most cases, effort and work is what brings promotion and title to one's life. But my blueberry pie diet ensured that position was more important than the pursuit. I found more value in the finished product than the preparation process. Now I never struggled with the concept of effort, persistence, and arduous work to earn a position, for I was driven to move toward the top. I just knew that a title would bring more value to my life.

My father and I were in the perfect business to feed this need. The service industry operates best when there is a hierarchical system, and we owned and managed restaurants. In about every restaurant I managed, worked, or owned, there were at least eight management positions with up to 100 employees. At one time while managing a restaurant in Kissimmee, Florida, I had nearly 150 people working underneath me.

Fast forward to the restaurant in Key West, and I had an average of 80 employees with a management staff of 8. The nature of the food service business, if you want to have a chance at being successful, is to be hands on. There is no success in running your restaurant from your couch at home. Being at the restaurant constantly did garner success, as we did win some awards from corporate over the years. The same was true for the cocaine business. (I hate calling it a business, but that is how it is being defined in this book.)

In each business you had to make yourself available, and I loved being the one people went to with their problems. Naturally this is the way it works in most any company. I have learned that as you move higher up and get paid more, you are getting paid to solve problems. But the position or title became a promised land for me. Bottom line, there was a sense of entitlement that came with earning a position—not entitlement as far as the perks that might come with the position, but rather the sense that I had earned that role. I liked the sense that because of my efforts alone, I had achieved a certain level of success.

I worked with a successful contractor some years ago who had built a good company, and he had all the stuff that came with wealth. I mentioned to him one day "God sure has blessed you here," to which he replied, "God? God did not have anything to do with this. I built this company." Looking back, I had the same mentality. Titles had provided a false sense of provision for what I desperately needed in my heart.

The apostle Paul reminds us, *"In whose case the god of this world has blinded the minds of the unbelieving so that they will not see the light of the gospel of the glory of Christ, who is the image of God,"* (2 Corinthians 4:4). The disease of "me, myself, and I" never has God as one of its symptoms. Pleasure, power, and position enjoyed and employed without God simply makes one their own god. Satan is the master of allowing one to achieve success, as long as you stay self-focused and you're for his work.

I am not knocking titles or positions completely. Obviously there is a connection between skill level and positions in any company or organization. Usually the higher up you look in a company's structure, the more talent you see in any given area. Great CFOs do not necessarily make great CEOs, and the CEO would not make a great CFO. Talent and skill does make a difference. However, when titles and positions become a promised land, the tools that built your success become less valuable and are often tabled.

My son James is a carpenter. He has his own framing business, and he is successful and doing great, but it has been a learning curve. His step-grandfather was an extremely successful builder. He started in the HVAC business not long after World War II. He went on to build houses, subdivisions, strip centers, hotels, and such. He used to say the biggest thing he ever built was his bank account. My son loved his step-grandfather and, in many ways, wanted to be just like him in his success while at the same time remaining true to himself. He would often say, "Dad, I want to get what Popeye (their name for their grandfather) has." My son saw all that wealth had brought to his grandfather and grandmother.

But here is what James did not see: the 30–50 years of work, talent, and skill that went into what James witnessed. It is like picking up a book on someone's success and only reading the last chapter. When position becomes your promised land, you forget about all the previous chapters, for you have focused only on the last chapter of the book. I am pleased to say that today with Christ, my son is allowing God to write the chapters.

When one forgets (or does not know) who gave them their success, they will begin to substitute other behaviors and thought processes that bring about a collapse.

Now we all know of some fabulously wealthy folks with big titles who do not recognize God. They seem to build wealth and never falter. But remember what the Lord said:

"Do not store up for yourselves treasures on earth, where moth and rust destroy, and where thieves break in and steal. But store up for yourselves treasures in heaven, where neither moth nor rust destroys, and where thieves do not break in or

steal; for where your treasure is, there your heart will be also," (Matthew 6:19-21).

Everything you credit to yourself here on earth will be left right here on earth when you die. Everything you own will belong to someone else someday.

We have all known people who have allowed their title to go to their head and then they begin to crumble. I had arrived at that place. In my search to fill a void in my heart, I inserted myself.

Learning a New Definition

As my faith grew, God did some of His best work in my life by teaching me about position. I began to see that the Lord is not concerned about our position—at least not as in title in a company structure. Rather, our Lord is focused on the position, as in place, in which He has placed us. It is the actual physical place, the position where we find ourselves on this earth, that is important. If there happens to be a title that goes with the physical designation, then know God gave you the place and title.

One of my first great discoveries as a Christian was the promise that God has a place and purpose just for me. Christ beautifully paints this picture for us as He uses the term "body" to refer to His church. Each believer is positioned perfectly in His body, the Church. And only God knows how to position His body. He knows where to place His people to best impact the world for His glory. Look at what the Holy Spirit led the apostle Paul to write to the Corinthian church:

"For just as the body is one and yet has many parts, and all the parts of the body, though they are many, are one body, so also is Christ. For by one Spirit we were all baptized into one body, whether Jews or Greeks, whether slaves or free, and we

were all made to drink of one Spirit. For the body is not one part, but many. If the foot says, "Because I am not a hand, I am not a part of the body," it is not for this reason any less a part of the body. And if the ear says, "Because I am not an eye, I am not a part of the body," it is not for this reason any less a part of the body. If the whole body were an eye, where would the hearing be? If the whole body were hearing, where would the sense of smell be? But now God has arranged the parts, each one of them in the body, just as He desired." (1 Corinthians 12:12-18).

Simply stated, the left foot works best on the end of the left leg, not connected to the right wrist. The body is one, though the parts are different and in various places. It is a unified body with diversity. There is unity, not uniformity. God's positioning of His "parts of the body" is diverse, but perfect in its placement.

Wherever you find yourself, you have found your mission field. If you are waiting to get the role of a teacher, ministry leader, choir leader, deacon, elder, or even a higher position at work before you get busy with Christ, you have become Pharisaical in attitude. Your attitude will remain the same, even when you finally get to where you desire.

The dream for a young Jewish boy during Jesus' day was to become a Pharisee. Years of study, memorizing scripture, and faithfully following God's law were pursued with honest intent. But the poison of power and position destroyed their ministry. Jesus recognized this issue in the Pharisees. Our Lord said in Luke 20:46-47, *"'Beware of the scribes, who like to walk around in long robes, and love personal greetings in the marketplaces, and chief seats in the synagogues and places of honor at banquets, who devour widows' houses, and for appearance's sake offer long prayers. These will receive all the more condemnation.'"*

So often in today's world we have seen the same scenario. Often, I believe, people of God have been led to build a ministry machine that serves God mightily, only to eventually become so self-enamored with their success, position, and popularity that they begin to use God to feed the machine, which is one's self.

Why did the Pharisees serve themselves? Why did they hate Jesus? They were afraid to lose their titles and positions of authority, for their value was in their title.

Have you ever known someone who had to take a demotion? Someone who went from the rank and file to management, and then back to the ranks? It can be a struggle.

I remember my early days of prison when a fellow brother in Christ shared this verse with me: *"But the greatest of you shall be your servant. Whoever exalts himself shall be humbled, and whoever humbles himself shall be exalted,"* (Matthew 23:11–12). I'll never forget that man. He was humble, he was kind, and he was a servant, even right there in prison.

As the scriptures began to take on life inside my heart, I was able to see God at work with clarity. I reflected on Len, his wife, and others at that little church in Sugarloaf Key, and I saw the beauty of their walk in Christ as they each knew they were positioned by the Lord.

Self-Entitlement

In my pursuit of a promised land, I officially caught the disease of self-entitlement. Without Christ, I always felt deserving of what I possessed rather than seeing things as a gift from God. The buck started and stopped with me.

Self-entitlement began with Lucifer. What was his problem? He wanted a title; he wanted the position that belonged to God. Isaiah records Lucifer's words: *"'But you said in your heart, "I will ascend to heaven; I will raise my throne above the stars of God, And I will sit on the mount of assembly In the recesses of the north. I will ascend above the heights of the clouds; I will make myself like the Most High."'"* (Isaiah 14:13–14).

A self-focus, which dismisses God, always leaves one with a position and purpose struggle. We see this further in Satan's history as Ezekiel reminds us,

"You were in Eden, the garden of God; Every precious stone was your covering: The ruby, the topaz and the diamond; the beryl, the onyx and the jasper; The lapis lazuli, the turquoise and the emerald; And the gold, the workmanship of your settings and sockets, was in you. On the day that you were created They were prepared. You were the anointed cherub who covers, And I placed you there. *You were on the holy mountain of God; You walked in the midst of the stones of fire."* (Ezekiel 28:13–14).

Lucifer had a position that was a result of God positioning him just where He wanted him. God created him for a specific role. But just like the ole dragon, if your definition of position is skewed, you will be unhappy and fight against God. Remember Jesus' observation of the scribes and Pharisees in Matthew 23:1–4:

"Then Jesus spoke to the crowds and to His disciples, saying: 'The scribes and the Pharisees have seated themselves in the chair of Moses. Therefore, whatever they tell you, do and comply with it all, but do not do as they do; for they say things and do not do them. *And they tie up heavy burdens and lay them on people's shoulders, but they themselves are unwilling to move them with so much as their finger.'"*

Nothing but entitlement all related to their position.

Back in Key West, the more the cocaine trade grew, the

more arrogant I became. Though it was a business that was supposed to be stealthy in operation, I found myself increasingly enjoying the secret notoriety I was receiving. For something that was supposed to be relegated to only whispers amongst certain folks, I frankly enjoyed the word getting around. The stigma of being a gangster was filling holes in my heart, for as the cocaine business grew, authority increasingly became a promised land.

However, the restaurant began to suffer. Intentional involvement in sin always clouds and dirties other areas of life. Number one, my role as a father was damaged. I was a good provider, but I was kidding myself thinking I could hold onto secret sin without it impacting my God-given role. My role as a husband was anything but a Godly husband. It seemed everything but the cocaine business began to suffer. I was spending less and less time at home and in the restaurant. The pursuit of the wrong promised land had me blinded. The apostle Paul reminds us as he speaks of Satan, *"In whose case the god of this world has blinded the minds of the unbelieving so that they will not see the light of the gospel of the glory of Christ, who is the image of God."* (2 Corinthians 4:4).

In the first sentence of Daniel 8:25, the prophet Daniel nails it on the head speaking of Satan: *"And through his shrewdness, He will make deceit a success by his influence ... "*

There it is again: self-deception at work. When we forget where things come from, we tie our self-worth to an entitlement mentality. We become the search engine for meaning and purpose. In doing so, we continually find other things to provide our needs. It is a constant search to provide for oneself. Just the opposite is biblically true: I am positioned on earth to simply be a steward.

Stop for a moment and read Matthew's recording of the parable of the talents in Matthew 25:14–30. God gives and positions, and He expects His children to be faithful stewards. That faithfulness begins in recognizing the origination of all we are and all we possess.

Reflect on your physical body, or the tree in your backyard; none of your body parts or the limbs on those trees have to manipulate or strive to stay alive. They simply stay connected to the body. What a beautiful promise from our Lord.

Obvious Observation

Now, obviously, just as in previous chapters, where there is nothing fundamentally wrong with pleasure or power, there is certainly nothing wrong with being a person positioned at the top of your job, group, club, company, team etc. There is nothing nefarious about working smart and hard to make your way up the corporate ladder with a goal of achieving a new title or position. We see that more money is spent on upper management than the receptionist, and a person's abilities make them more valuable to their company. Positions and titles work well in the workplace, as ultimately someone needs to be in charge to keep things operating smoothly.

However, that position does nothing to create more value in God's eyes. Nowhere in scripture does Christ recognize someone as being more important because of their title. Luke reminds us, *"'God is not one to show partiality,'"* (Acts 10:34c). In simpler words, God gives no preference to someone based on title, power, or wealth.

I cannot but help think of Warren Buffet who, after giving away nearly 85 percent of his fortune, said at a donation ceremony at the New York Public Library, "There is more than one way to get to heaven, but this is a great way." What average person can compete with that? I hope and pray Mr. Buffet finds the one and only way to God.

Arriving at the Wrong Promised Land

I enjoyed my title during the cocaine years. I loved it when the people around me referred to me as "El Jefe." Of course, the Spanish word simply means "the one in charge." But in certain circles, it was used in the drug world to refer to the one at the top. I was a long way from an "El Jefe" as we see in the movies and news today, but nevertheless, I liked the title. As far as South Florida went, I was the one who possessed the top title.

I loved it when our supplier referred to me as El Jefe. I loved walking into bars, clubs, or restaurants, and having other dealers nod or say hello. As secretive as we tried to keep the cocaine smuggling, people talk, and more and more people knew what I was doing.

As time went on, the attention I received allowed me access to clubs, hidden casinos, and immediate seating at restaurants. Of course, money always was the motivator for people. I had plenty of it, and people knew I would part with large sums of it. My blindness and pride told me our power, influence, money, and reputation would keep us safe, no matter how many people knew. My dad always assured me he had my back.

The position of authority was an ego boost for me, and it was feeding my heart's deception by the spoonful.

I was sitting at a bar in Coconut Grove, Miami with the crew that helped me during those smuggling years. It was a wonderful place on the harbor. Dad had flown to Miami himself, and we were able to trade dollars for cocaine and deliver it to Dad all within one hour. We were done for the day, no long trip back and forth to Nashville. We had lots of money, and I was going to spend plenty. Spending money was an ego boost.

We were there for several hours, picking up the tab for others as we always did. By the time we were ready to leave, the tab had passed the $1500 mark. So I asked the server for the tab, but she said the tab was paid. I thought one of the guys had stolen my thunder and paid the tab, but they assured me they had not. So we got up to leave. As we ambled to the car, Ralph and a friend walked up and told me, "It's on us today."

I had arrived in the promised land of position, for it was my role in the cocaine trade that paid that bar tab. I was proud of that moment.

My arrogance, blindness, and hypocrisy were building. I had even accepted a position on the Police Athletic League board of directors. I had been asked to participate in business clubs and meetings, asked to sponsor events, and a whole list of other honorable tasks. Of course, people around town thought that I was simply a successful restaurant operator, and that the restaurant was producing huge profits. Thus, Mike, the owner of a large family chain restaurant, was becoming well-known in town. What a mixed bag—some people saw an honest, hardworking businessman, while others saw me as a cocaine smuggler. It was the best of both worlds, I thought.

Learning a New Definition

As I have grown in Christ, He has demonstrated to me repeatedly that it is not the position I possess, but rather the place in which the Lord has positioned me. God's teaching methods are simply "out of this world."

In the few years before prison, while under house arrest and the watchful eye of the federal government, I experienced events that demonstrated this truth. So often the unexpected happened because of being positioned in the right place. The correct positioning always came about as a work of God. I have never foreseen or planned His work in my life. That is His business.

This manifested itself in many ways: how the Lord cared for my family when I was in prison, how the Lord protected me when I was away, and then the job I took when leaving prison. But as these events were taking place over three years, there was also a stripping down of who I thought I was. I was stripped of every title I had owned—or thought I owned—and left naked before the Lord. No longer was I the owner of a popular restaurant, or the son of a well-known and respected businessman. No longer would I own a nice house on the water, nor would I be the guy with a Lear jet at his beck and call. I was no longer asked to sponsor fundraisers, nor was I "generous Mike" who gave away hundred-dollar bills like they were pennies.

None of that existed anymore; my position now was one of a felon and soon-to-be convicted money launderer in a drug conspiracy. The proverbial fall from grace had taken place. Little did I know that I had fallen into grace, and God was going to strip me down so as to clothe me in His righteousness.

Which brings the words of 2 Corinthians 5:21 to mind: *"He made Him who knew no sin to be sin in our behalf, so that we might become the righteousness of God in Him."* God has imputed unto the child of God the sinless life of Christ and His righteousness, and imparted unto the believer the grace by which to live the Christian life. But though a sinner is transformed instantly into a saint, the work of the sanctification process is just beginning.

The apostle Paul explains in an often-misinterpreted scripture, *"So then, my beloved, just as you have always obeyed, not as in my presence only, but now much more in my absence, work out your own salvation with fear and trembling,"* (Philippians 2:12).

This is often interpreted as the responsibility of the believer to work for their salvation: work to earn it and work to keep it. However, Paul is simply pointing out the direct responsibility of the believer to respond in obedience to Christ to bring one's sanctification to fruition. So as God had stripped me of all the positions and titles I possessed, He took me on a journey that is forever etched in my heart, and that I often share when I'm speaking at events. The result: while in prison, I learned the true definition of "position" and the continued blessings of the true Promised Land.

Placed In the Valley

After my sentencing on February 2, 2001, I was taken from the courtroom to a jail in Bowling Green, KY. From Bowling Green I was moved to Mason, TN, to Atlanta, GA, eventually ending up in Petersburg, VA. Not long after landing in Petersburg, I immediately set my heart on my Bible study and learning about Christ. I made a few friends and got involved in the church. My years between my surrender to Christ and my sentencing had been spent in study and some teaching, but I did not have the time that God was now affording me in prison.

I found the Bible exciting and fascinating, and I became a consumer of all it had to offer. I knew prison would not be easy, and that I was going to walk through some valleys, but my lawyer had told me to "focus on exiting the valley a better person than the way I had entered the valley." Thus I was focused on allowing God to change my heart.

Like many new Christians, I just knew God had saved me for some magnificent work. Surely, God had been waiting on me to get to Petersburg to rally the saints and be the catalyst for a great prison revival. Who really believes that? No one, but I did for a while. Remember what EGO always does—it Edges God Out.

There was a lesson I would quickly learn, and it came in the form of a whisper in my heart. Though I was a mostly new Christian and ignorant of God's ways, I did feel energized and wanted to start Bible studies and prayer times in the prison dorms. So I submitted a request to the chaplain and asked for permission to order the *Experiencing God* study and start a four-night-a-week Bible study in the dorm. I envisioned 4–5 guys meeting in the hallway, or outside at a picnic table, or even in a utility closet—wherever we could meet. On top of that, I was convinced the chaplain would be overjoyed to have such a zealous Christian inmate amongst the population. I just knew that God sent me there to be his Moses.

Yeah, right.

I will never forget when I was called to appear in the chaplain's office. I ran to his office with ego and excitement; I could not wait to tell him of all my great ideas and how he could rest assured in my "position" as leader of a small group. Yep, even here, I was looking for a position again.

The moment I stepped into his office, without any small talk, he firmly told me that this could not happen. He said he "was too busy at the other prisons there on the compound." He did not have time to manage us or check on us daily or even weekly. On top of that, he informed me that there was a rule that four or more inmates could not gather for a meeting, prayer, study, or any other gathering unless it was a sanctioned event by the prison and okayed by the warden. End of discussion.

I must admit, I was angry. How could God allow the prison chaplain, of all people, to stop a Bible study from taking place? I walked away frustrated, convinced that Satan had the chaplain in his pocket.

Saturday came, and I headed out to the prison track—a gravel and dirt circle where guys would walk and jog—and I planted myself on a set of old wooden bleachers that had been there for decades. I liked the bleacher spot for reading and study. There were trees that shaded most of the seating, and there was a good view of the track and softball field. Yes, there was a softball field and track, not to mention a free weight area as well as an outside basketball court. It wasn't the "Club Fed" like the rumors say, but it was a prison with opportunities for sports, activities ... anything to keep the inmates busy.

On this particular May Saturday, the sun was shining, the breeze blowing, and I was all alone on the bleachers with my Bible and journal. I settled in and started to pray, which had become my habit before reading the scriptures. It was during that prayer that I began to voice my consternation to God about the inability to get anything going. I complained of the chaplain, reminding God that He had even allowed me to teach a Sunday school class before I went to prison. I continued and reminded God of all I was trying to do and all I wanted to do.

Then there came the whisper. I am not sure I heard a voice, but clear as a bell, in my head, I heard these words: "Mike, I appreciate what you are trying to do for me, but I am the One who will do it though you. I have placed you there." I scribbled those words in my journal as fast as I could. I sat for an hour, praying and meditating, then got up and went to the dorm for the 4:00 count time. (At 4:00 P.M. in every federal prison, the inmates are required to be standing in their room or cell, so as to be counted.)

As I headed back to the dorm, I mulled over the statement

"I have placed you there." I knew I had heard from God, yet it was another head-scratcher.

I got back to my cubicle: about eight feet by six feet, a tad smaller than the prison cell in Atlanta, with one bunk bed, two stacked lockers, and a single desk. But when I arrived, there was a letter on the desk. It had come in on Friday's mail call and only now had made it to my cubicle.

The letter was from Ms. Anita. I had met her at the church in Key West, but she had since moved to California. She was a delightful mature believer. She said she felt led by God to go on a fast, and that she was to write me and ask me to fast along with her. She stated that she was fasting and praying that I would be open to receive what God was doing, and going to do, in my life. I thought I already knew that answer—go to prison, study the Bible, and become a teacher.

But Ms. Anita was proposing a version of the Daniel fast, as Daniel practiced in Daniel 10:2-3. Ms. Anita suggested forty days. I opened my Bible and read Daniel. My first thought was, *No way. Fasting is for the "over the top" Christians who need to lose weight.* But then I thought how Ms. Anita was a thin lady, and she was so humble. So I read Daniel again. I knew that fast would be difficult in prison. I did not have my own fridge nor access to a grocery store.

So I prayed over the weekend and read her letter a dozen times. When Monday morning arrived, I began my fast. I would only eat the vegetables served in the chow hall, and I would eat two apples a day. Drinking only water was not an issue, as that was all I drank in prison. I instantly became a hit with a few of my buddies as I gave away the meat, bread, pasta, and dessert of every meal.

Ms. Anita had shared that during meal times or times of hunger, I should be in prayer. So that Monday, I wrote "Day One" in my journal. The first week was difficult. I had headaches, and my stomach kept telling me to eat, but my heart was locked in. And that's when God stepped in.

On day thirteen, I got a call to go to the main desk to speak with the guard on duty.

"Hardy, pack up your stuff. You are leaving tomorrow," he told me.

"What?" I responded. "Where am I going? Why am I being moved?"

"That is none of your business," was the terse response.

Of course, that is how it goes in prison.

So I went to my cubicle and packed up my belongings in the prison-provided duffel bag. I took it back downstairs and turned it over to the guard. That would be the last I would see my property for four months. When you leave a prison, they clothe you, shackle your hands and feet, and send you off with nothing else.

So on day fourteen of my fast, I was on a prison bus headed to Atlanta. In Atlanta, I decided to continue my fast. I had no access to fruit. The only food was the three meals a day provided, so I ate only the non-meat and non-starch items. I am not able to fully explain, but prayer had me focused— thus I stayed the course.

On day 21, I was driven to the airport, and myself and 100 other shackled inmates boarded a plane. The next stop: Oklahoma City. When the plane landed in Oklahoma City, it taxied to the end of the runway and the boarding bridge was extended to meet the plane. One step off the plane and we were in the federal prison, right there at the airport.

It was the middle of the night when I was taken to the seventh floor and brought to a cell. "You're assigned to the bottom bunk," the officer told me. As the cell door swung open, the first thing I saw was a six-foot wall of muscle laying on the bottom bunk. I got my rear up on the top bunk and I stayed there until day 38 of the fast.

That wall of muscle turned out to be Larry, a convicted murderer who had been in prison for twenty-three years. I became fast friends with Larry. He loved eating the extra food off my trays and I was no challenge to him in the endless chess games in which we engaged. (Full disclosure: I threw many games I thought I might win. You just do not know about people, especially in prison.)

I stayed focused on the fast. I was no longer hungry, and there seemed to be so much more clarity as I studied the Bible. In every prison, I always found a Bible available. That was special, and it meant a lot that people donated to that cause. I became less focused on myself. I knew the Lord was with me. I could feel His presence, and at times when I struggled with sadness, I simply read the promises of scripture and reminded myself of what Jesus had said in Matthew 28:20b: "'... and behold, I am with you always, to the end of the age.'"

On day thirty-eight of the fast, I was told that I was leaving for Miami. This was the first time I knew where I was headed, though I still do not know why. On day thirty-nine, I was flown to Miami and bussed to the Miami Federal Detention Center. I was placed in "the hole"—solitary—and told I would be leaving in the morning. I knew now I was being taken back to Key West, but for what reason, I had no idea. But God knew.

On Day 40, the last day of the fast, I had woken early, and two US Marshals put me in their car and drove about 100 mph down the highway headed toward the Florida Keys. It was an exhilarating day, as I enjoyed the car ride. I was seeing so much of what I had seen for years. I felt nervous, but there was a calmness and peace that overrode my anxiousness. I knew not what was going to take place, but I did know the One who knew everything. I had memorized the King James Version of Isaiah 26:3 while on my fast: *"Thou wilt keep* him *in perfect peace,* whose *mind* is *stayed* on Thee: *because he trusteth in Thee."* I have never had that truth fail me.

By the end of day 40, at about 8 PM, I arrived at the Key West jail. I was placed in the very pod (a large room with bunk beds and sections housing about forty men) where I had participated in Bible study 3 1/2 years earlier, before I had left Key West, eventually heading to prison. I knew God was at work.

Now that the fast was over, I was looking forward to eating some extra food, even though it was jail food. I was always thankful for what I received and never complained about my provisions while in prison. Truth be told, people in American prisons live a lifestyle far above billions of people in the world, as there was always running water, a shower, three meals a day, a bed, and protection from the elements.

Chaplain Judy came to the pod the next morning, now 41 days since the fast began. I had known her when I lived in Key West, and I had participated with her in jail Bible studies back in 1997 and 1998. She asked me, "Mike, what can I bring you to help reach this dorm for Christ?"

I asked for a stack of Bibles, some pencils, and paper. I had them within one hour. After receiving the material, I stood amid the dorm and shouted out, "If anyone wants to participate in a daily Bible study, I will be leading each morning." I did not know what to expect. But my brother-in-law was there with me, which reassured me. He had been part of the business, and he was brought back to Key West from a different prison as well. He had given his life to Christ, too. It was a blessing to be there with him, as he was an all-in type guy. He did not do things 90 percent; he was full-on in his commitment. So I told the chaplain "I know two of us will be there."

The next morning, I found a stainless-steel table and benches (all welded to the ground) and sat myself down with a stack of ten Bibles that Chaplain Judy had brought me. My brother-in-law joined me, and three other guys showed up. Two of the guys would soon be leaving for prison, and the third guy was near the end of his six-month sentence for a DUI. Despite how short their stay would be, we started in the book of John. That first week saw only 3–5 men participate. The people would sometimes change out, but the numbers stayed about the same.

The contrast between here and Petersburg was clear. The door had seemed to slam in my face in Petersburg. But in this jail, the door had opened, and I had not been the one to open it. I knew God was in control. How else can you explain me starting a fast that I hadn't even wanted to do, and on day forty, ending up in the very town where all my crime had originated? And not only that—in the same dorm where I had first read the Bible in a prison setting?

Embracing Where You're Positioned

In the meantime, I was eating again, and I was enjoying it. As I said, I would not complain about the food—but I often would have liked a second helping. I was blessed to have some money on my prison canteen account, which was a prison grocery store of sorts. With it I could order some honey buns, pop tarts, chips, and such. My friend Scott and a few other Christian men kept a few dollars on my account.

Since day one I had noticed a particular guy in the corner bunk. He had the bunk to himself; no one slept above him. He was big—6' 9", 280 lbs. He was a White guy, his tattoos told me he was a neo-Nazi or a white supremacist. He had the tear drops, the spider web, and lightning bolts on his chest. He had words and symbols on his body which told everyone his life had been one of hatred. I noticed he stayed to himself. He was not popular—out of the forty guys in the pod, thirty of them were non-white. The hateful marks he bore on his skin surely made him an enemy here.

He mostly stayed on his bunk and read. He always took his food tray to his bunk and ate there, never sitting with the others. I noticed that he did not ever eat the hamburgers or chicken that were served, choosing to always throw them away. Now, in jail culture, if you do not want something, you either give it away or, more likely, you trade for something. You know, *I give you my hamburger, and you give me your fries and cookie, or something akin to that.*

So after observing him for a good while, I decided to approach this guy. I would introduce myself, discuss food, and mention the Bible study, although I was already convinced he would not be interested. I've found that so often we approach the opportunity to share our faith having already decided for the other person that they are not interested.

It was like the time one of my best friends, Mike (yep, another Mike), got a job right out of college selling Kirby vacuums. I could not believe the price of those vacuums, and I do not think Mike could either. He worked hard, but sales just did not happen. Eventually, he was convinced before he even knocked on a single door that no one wanted that vacuum. I am afraid that too many Christians have that mindset—they think they have something no one is interested in, but they would find that that's not true if they would only open their mouths properly and in love. (By the way, Mike never gave up. He went into a new business adventure, and he is extremely successful today.)

So I approached this big fellow with a vacuum seller's mentality, certain he wouldn't want what I had to offer, all due to his appearance. "Hello, my name is Mike. I am sure you have noticed that I sleep just a few bunks over from you."

"Yeah, okay. My name is Robert. What do you want?"

"I could not help but notice that you do not eat your burgers or chicken, and I was wondering if you wanted to trade."

"Trade for what?"

I was ready with my response. "Well, I have honey buns and some other candy if that would be interesting to you."

Robert stood up. "I like the honey buns with the icing."

"No problem," I replied. "I only have the non-icing buns now, but I will order the iced honey buns for next week."

Robert simply said, "Deal."

Then I continued, "I am also leading a Bible study each morning, I am sure you have seen us, but you are invited."

"No, that's okay," he replied. "I have plenty of Bibles that I read right here on my bunk." He pointed to a small stack of books under his bed. I noticed that what he was referring to as "Bibles" were actually a collection of several different faith books; Robert had a Bible, the book of Mormon, the Quran, and a book on Mysticism lined up under his bunk. But I was not about to correct his definition of all of those books being "Bibles."

I told him, "I will see you on hamburger or chicken day," and I walked fifteen feet back to my bunk.

He was in his own world, but I sensed a sadness and darkness when I talked to him. I wondered, "Lord, did you bring me here to meet Robert?"

Three mornings later, I had just announced the start of the study when, with a loud thump, Robert dropped his Bible on the table and sat down. The second he sat, two of the four

Black guys at the table got up and walked away. Robert got up to leave.

I quickly interjected. "Robert, this table is for everyone who wants to learn about Jesus. That includes you." He paused, then he sat back down.

I sensed a tension with some of the guys. Robert had lived a life of hatred and bigotry. He knew he bore the testimony of his beliefs in the marks on his body. He knew the deeds of his heart, and that those deeds were on full display. He knew that danger was always just moments away.

As the weeks went on, Robert came to every study. I came to learn more about him. He was twenty-eight years old; he had been in and out of prison since age seventeen. He was in jail now for hurting someone badly in a fight. He said he had been out of prison for just a few months when he was attacked. He defended himself, the other person went to the hospital, and he was arrested and charged with aggravated assault as a habitual offender. The district attorney was offering him fifteen years.

As we began to talk, Robert and I became friends. It was an awkward position to be in, as I found myself being shunned by some of the folks of color.

During this time, a local pastor and some of the men who had been instrumental in my coming to faith were visiting me each week. In fact, the pastor was allowed access into the dorm and often had permission to take me out of the dorm to a private room. I enjoyed the study time immensely. I had shared the story about Robert with one of my visiting friends, Jim. Three days later, Robert received his own study Bible in the mail. I told the pastor, and he began to take Robert out with me so we could study together. Robert's coldness began changing to a warmth.

After about a month, I noticed Robert at the book rack in

the dorm; he was placing all those other "Bibles", as he called them, back on the shelf. Then on a Saturday afternoon, Robert asked the pastor, "Pastor, can I be forgiven? If so, I want to be forgiven and invite Christ into my heart."

After an hour or so of discussing Christ's forgiveness, how it is applied and how it is accepted, Robert got down on that concrete floor and prayed the most beautiful simple prayer. Both the pastor and I wept, and then Robert began to weep. He said, "I cannot remember the last time I cried."

As the next few weeks went on, Robert devoured the scriptures. He asked hundreds and hundreds of questions. He would even stay away from the Bible study some mornings to allow the other guys to participate. I was so excited watching his life transform. I remember speaking with my mother on the phone and telling her of what was happening there in the jail. I told her, "Mom, if they opened this jail up today and told me I could leave, I am not going anywhere, this is where God has POSITIONED me." I was learning the importance of position.

Then one afternoon, it finally happened. I always wondered if it would, and Robert thought the same. Robert was standing in our pod, talking with my brother-in-law and myself. I did not even see it coming. Three guys with bars of soap in socks came up behind Robert and started swinging. The first blows sounded like bowling balls hitting the ground with loud thuds. He covered himself, placing his elbows together and attempting to cover his face with his hands. There was nothing we could do; you cannot allow yourself to jump into a fight like that. The guard in the dorm was issuing the command to stop; when the fight continued, the call on the radio went out. In just forty-five seconds, five guards were running in the dorm, dispersing pepper spray, and calling out "Everyone on the ground!"

I will never forget watching Robert as he took those blows. He was a big, tough guy, but Robert's heart had been divinely changed. As they were beating him, he slowly walked himself into a corner and allowed them to continue to beat him. His skin and face was ripped open, his scalp was torn, and blood was everywhere. Yet Robert never lifted a hand. My brother-in-law and I were screaming at Robert to fight back, but Robert knew more of Christ at that moment than I had ever learned. Robert told the pastor later that he was praying for them as they beat him. The words of Matthew 5:44 filled Robert's mind and heart: *"'But I say to you, love your enemies and pray for those who persecute you.'"* How could he have done that? His heart was full, and Robert knew it.

They took the villains away, and they took Robert away. Little did I know that I was going to leave the jail and begin the slow travel process back to Petersburg the very next day. My time there was over. The guard told me to gather my things that evening of Robert's beating. A guard called the pastor and told him what happened and that I was leaving.

The next morning, just one hour before we left, the pastor walked into the dorm. Not knowing that he already knew the events of the previous evening, I ran to tell him.

"Pastor, I am so glad you are here. I am leaving today, but Robert was beat up yesterday; it was really bad, and he ... "

The pastor stopped me. "Mike, I already know. I was called, and I went to visit Robert this morning. He was in rough shape, but he will heal, and he told me to give you a message. He said to tell you that he is a follower of Christ now; no more fighting and hatred."

I welled up with tears. I never saw Robert again, but the pastor did. Amazingly, the DA dropped Robert's case. He got out of jail, and he joined the Key West Church of God. He joined the choir. He never missed church. He wore turtlenecks and long sleeves to cover his tattoos. He got to know the child he had fathered during his few months out of prison. His heart was radically changed. Then a cough took Robert to the doctor. Cancer had come calling, and Robert would be gone in eleven months. I can be certain I will see him again.

I will never forget the first time I shared that story with Judy. She commented, "What amazing love God had for Robert." She was right. I think of all the moving parts that pieced together to reach Robert. It started with me in prison, then Petersburg, the chaplain telling me no, God's whisper on the bleachers, Ms. Anita's letter, the 40-day fast, Atlanta, Oklahoma City, the exact dorm where I had been 31/2 years earlier, Chaplain Judy, my honey bun supply ... the list goes on. God cared about Robert so much that He knew how to position His people to reach Robert.

I always cry when telling this story, and even while writing it now. But it's not because Robert is gone, or that God used me, but rather because of how much love God had for Robert. God is at work positioning His people for His work. Take some time and read of Nehemiah again and how God positioned him to rebuild the walls of Jerusalem. Or refresh your memory of Joseph in the Old Testament, and how God's providence was at work giving Joseph a title that would position him to save his family and God's children.

Christ's presence in my life continues to reveal truths, here is one of my favorites: *"For we are His workmanship, created in Christ Jesus for good works, which God prepared beforehand so that we would walk in them,"* (Ephesians 2:10). God has a plan for you right where you are. Stay put and get busy; you are in His Promised Land.

Reflection Questions

1. How do you define position? How close is position tied to your value and perception of yourself? Do you crave authority?

2. Does your position give you a sense of entitlement? Why do you feel entitled? What do you feel you are entitled to?

3. Have you allowed authority to go to your head? What would your employees or fellow co-workers say?

4. Who gave you your job? Did God position you? Why are you where you are?

5. Who is God asking you to approach? What is stopping you?

6. Have you missed God's opportunities? How can you be better prepared for His plans and His work?

8

WHERE THE PROMISED LAND IS NOT FOUND—PERFORMANCE

About Performance

Performance would be my "chocolate pie." Truthfully, about any style chocolate pie or cake would suffice, but we do have our favorites.

Merriam Webster has multiple different definitions for performance. The first is: "the execution of an action."[14] However,

there is one that is better suited for me: "the action of representing a character in a play."

I have only been in one play my entire life; it was *The Wizard of Oz*, and I played the Tin Man. As the Tin Man, I hoped that my fourth grade acting skills convinced folks that they were on the yellow brick road. My mother had made a fabulous costume, and I had the Tin Man walk down pat.

But my performance didn't stop at *The Wizard of Oz*. I have secretly appeared in thousands of one-man shows over the years. Instead of trying to convince folks that I was something else, like I had done as the Tin Man, I labored to keep my identity hidden, willing to transform like a chameleon based on my surroundings. No, I did not wear a fake beard or wig, nor did I change my name. But I did disguise myself by working hard to hide the insecurity and emptiness that existed in my heart.

This insecurity wasn't born from any one event. It had grown over a long period of time. Of course, I have learned that my emptiness was first connected to the lack of a personal relationship with Christ, as there is no adequate infinite filling of the soul without Christ. Absent of God, one is left to existentialism—seeking to define oneself and to determine one's own future. The trouble with self-definition is that it is often flexible, constantly changing with the times. Additionally, a fluid definition of self will often provide others unfettered access to our emotions. We will often change our behavior—or put on a performance—to appease whoever is nearby.

My insecurity also arose from my unhealthy relationship with my father. Though life with my dad was not one of constant misery, I now look back and recognize that our attitudes and actions were dysfunctional. I never had peace about who I was. Whether it was on the tennis court, on the football field, or in the restaurant business, I just did not seem to measure up in his eyes. For three decades, if you had asked me, "Who are you?" I would have replied, "Ask my dad." For years I simply worked to keep him happy.

The result was a changing identity, which was exhausting. This practice brought me so close to abdicating my role as a father in my own home. Without any parental example of finding the Promised Land, my children were doomed to pursue their own illusions of fulfillment. The statistics are overwhelming; parents' actions are responsible for a child's faith formation—especially the father's. I learned as I studied God's word that the first Jesus any child meets is the one in their parents.

It is within that relationship that a child learns of love, mercy, grace, discipline, and obedience. It is the parent who first holds the child's hand and prays, the parent who prays to the invisible Father, who speaks of Christ, and who sets the example of a steadfast life standing on the Rock. It is the parents' responsibility to lead the child to Christ—to participate in the molding and unfolding of the child. It is in the home where a child learns that it is okay to be who he or she is: a child of God. Too many children today are constantly putting on a performance to please their parents. Just last night, I heard the story of a local twelve-year-old who felt unloved and abused by his dad; the boy hung himself. There is so much pressure in the world today to perform. I thank the Lord each morning for two children who live in a saved relationship with Jesus Christ and are grateful that their parents led them to know Christ.

Pressure to Perform

Dad sent me a Lou Holtz quote years ago that read, "If what you did yesterday seems big, you haven't done anything today."[15] I did not hear coach Holtz deliver that quote, but I have listened to him speak, via the internet, many times. There is no question that he meant to inspire his players to press on and not rest in yesterday's achievement. However, for me, it was a reminder that I needed to be different than who I was. It instilled a need to constantly reinvent myself. The drive to appease that which was outside of me was a steady work.

Bottom line: there is so much pressure in the world today to perform. It is not just for kids or social media junkies, but for all walks of life. In my life, it was the pursuit of the right performance that would drive me to grand selfishness and criminal behavior. Was all of life like that? No—along life's journey I did do a few things well, even earning accolades as a reward for good thinking and hard work. There is certainly nothing unsound about that, but those things never filled my heart with any staying power.

Here is a math equation to help explain. My great friend Pastor Josh shared these with me. Jesus + something = nothing, while Jesus + nothing = everything. The "something" of the first equation is our self-sufficiency which, when we try to bring to our relationship with Christ, results in a tarnished and less-than result at best. We add no value to Christ. In contrast, when He does the work, and we trust in Him by fully surrendering to Him, all His provisions are available. Remember the promise in Philippians 4:19, *"And my God will supply all your needs according to His riches in glory in Christ Jesus."* God does all the providing.

Seek out the Truth

Eventually I was running the Florida part of the drug operation. I would receive the marching orders from Dad, then my crew and I were off to the races. I liked what we were doing for two reasons: we were good at what we did, and it made Dad happy.

Here is the crazy part: during those drug years, my dad and I got along great. I even told the Assistant US Attorney, "Those years were some of the best years I ever had with my dad." I will never forget the look he and my attorney gave me. My attorney simply put his arm around my shoulder and said, "You were deceived."

He was correct. I was deceived by myself, primarily. I had bought the devil's lie—I was taking a shortcut. Looking back, it is amazing the effort and hard work that went into pursuing the flesh. I am convinced that many folks will enter Hell exhausted, with sweat-stained shirts and perspiration on their foreheads. A person who is outside of a personal relationship with Christ will exhaust themself in attempting to find meaning and purpose; it will not be found in a fallen world.

Here is where the promises of scripture are so vitally important to the follower of Christ—especially the new believer. There is no combating identity crises or lies unless one knows TRUTH. Further, even a believer will struggle with an identity crisis when attempting to keep one foot in Egypt, biblically synonymous with sin and the lure of pleasure, power and possessions, and one foot in the Promised Land. This Christian, unknowingly perhaps, is putting on a performance. As my friend Brooks says, "They have one mask on at church and another one on in the bar."

The pursuit of the right performance in others was crucial to sustaining my identity dilemma. Simply put, when one is doing wrong, it is nice to be surrounded by affirming, like-minded folks. Any pushback from someone outside that supportive inner group was met with disdain and pride.

Here is a perfect example. Not long after the restaurant in

South Florida opened in 1992, it became obvious that we
were going to be a daily stop for some folks. We had customers who ate with us 4–5 days a week for years. One such customer was Mrs. Pat. She was in her early 80's and had just recently lost her husband. We became great friends. She visited
the restaurant daily, and we talked about life and memories.
I tried my best to never miss a chance to sit with her, even if
for a moment. I loved her company, and she enjoyed mine.
She was so wise and had a knack for seeing things from a different angle.

One day, a fellow who was selling us kilos walked into the
restaurant. There was not a problem with him being there,
but we would not normally meet in public. Some folks' rep-
utations were not as hidden as they thought, and I wanted
to be careful. Oh, how naïve (and arrogant) I was, as rumors
had begun swirling about my drug involvement as well.

I visited with my buddy for a few minutes before he left. As
he walked out the door, I saw Mrs. Pat. She caught my eye and
asked me to sit down with her.

"Do you know who that man is and what he does?" she
asked me.

I replied as innocently as I could. "Sure, he's a pretty regular customer. He owns a small business in town."

But Mrs. Pat was not going for that answer. I could tell she
knew his reputation as a cocaine trafficker. In my mind, I was
wondering how this sweet senior lady could possibly know
this guy, but before I could ask, she said, "Don't worry how
I know, but know that I am telling you the truth: keep your
distance."

Man, did I put on a performance for her. "No, that's not
right. He is a great customer. I even shop at his store. Mrs.
Pat, you have it wrong."

I am ashamed to say my relationship with her went downhill

after that. She stopped coming in as often, and she told one of my managers, "I'm not sure who Mike is anymore."

Wow is all I can say as I look back. But at the time, I thought she was out of line. Why? Because she did not agree with my false analysis of my friend nor my performance. I am forever grateful now that Mrs. Pat was not a performer for me—she stuck to her guns.

To Perform or Not to Perform

God used a story in the Old Testament to speak to me about performance. It, along with the stories of Joseph and Daniel, became one of my go-to memories when dealing with the temptation to cave into pressure. I reckon we all have our favorite Bible stories, so here is one of mine, found in 1 Kings 22.

The story revolves around King Ahab and his ultimate demise. The previous chapters had revealed King Ahab's two victories over Syria. Surprisingly, though Ahab was a vile and wicked king, he still found favor with God. Chapter 22 picks up after three years of peace between the King of Israel and the King of Syria, Benhadad. The chapter begins with King Jehoshaphat of Judah coming to visit King Ahab.

After three years of calm, King Ahab decides it is time to fight against Syria once more. It's unbelievable how pride will keep you fighting. Right at the beginning, we have an immediate problem, as God did not send either king to fight against Syria. But nevertheless, King Ahab of Israel asks King Jehoshaphat of Judah to go to battle with him against Syria. Jehoshaphat does not have a problem with the invite, but he wants to inquire of the Lord before heading off to battle. (Smart move!) So Ahab goes to work stacking the deck.

First he parades out a group of four hundred false prophets

claiming that victory lays ahead. Then Zedekiah, the spokesperson for this evil group, prophecies of their victory, even placing a set of iron horns on his head and running in front of the king, supposedly emulating how his army will destroy and drive out the Syrians. But ole Jehoshaphat is not impressed nor persuaded—no performance from false prophets is going to change his standard. He asks, *"Is there no longer a prophet of the Lord here, that we may inquire of him?"* (verse 7).

Unenthusiastically, King Ahab confesses in verse eight, *"There is still one man by whom we may inquire of the Lord, but I hate him, because he does not prophesy* anything *good regarding me, but* only *bad. He is Micaiah the son of Imlah."* (verse 8). Often weak leaders, including believers, who are misusing their relationship with Christ will have animosity toward anyone who they perceive as disagreeing with them. So Ahab begrudgingly sends a messenger for Micaiah.

The messenger arrives and speaks to Micaiah, saying essentially, "Hey buddy, this is important to the king. He wants things to go his way, and he is trying to convince the King of Judah to go to war, so do not say anything bad against the king, and make sure you agree with the other false prophets." (verse 13, my paraphrase.)

So off to the king they go. Upon arrival, Micaiah says, *"As the Lord lives, whatever the Lord says to me, I shall speak it."* (verse 14).

Confident that Micaiah will perform for him, Ahab asks, "Shall we go against Ramoth-Gilead to battle?"

Micaiah answers sarcastically, "Sure, go ahead, you'll be victorious." (verse 15, my paraphrase.)

So an angry and frustrated Ahab admonishes Micaiah, saying, *"How many times must I make you swear that you will tell me nothing but the truth in the name of the Lord?"* (verse 16).

Now let me ask you something: does Ahab want *the truth* or *his way?* There are two sides: those that will lie and put on a performance for the king, and the single prophet who speaks truth with no performance. Ahab wants the yes-men around him to confirm his foolish decision to proceed without God. He has surrounded himself with folks who will agree to anything he says without disagreeing or pushing back. Ahab is surrounded by performers, who are content to dance on his puppet strings. Ahab needs this; he craves this. His very existence and self-worth are found in surrounding himself with folks who agree with him and perform for him.

But Micaiah, God's man, speaks. *"I saw all Israel Scattered on the mountains, Like sheep that have no shepherd."* (verse 17).

"I told you he never says anything good!" bellowed Ahab. (verse 18, my paraphrase.)

Finally, scripture reports that Micaiah saw a vision of God on His throne, surrounded by a heavenly host, where the Lord asked, *"'Who will entice Ahab to go up and fall at Ramoth-Gilead?' ...*

"Then a spirit came forward and stood before the Lord, and said, 'I will entice him.' And the Lord said to him, 'How?' And he said, 'I will go out and be a deceiving spirit in the mouths of all his prophets.' Then He said, 'You shall entice him, and you will also prevail. Go and do so.'" (verses 20a–22).

Let's pause for a moment—this is fascinating. God allows Satan (the father of lies) to speak through the false prophets and Ahab heads off into battle. Interesting, isn't it? God uses Satan. Far too many Christians believe God and Satan are on the same level, as if they are opposites. Really, nothing could be further from the truth. Satan, in some sense, is also God's servant. So read and remember, my friend: if you are determined to act against God, if you are determined to hear only the sound of like-minded voices, and if performance is what sways you, then God will let you go your way. But take note that going your own way often leads to disastrous results down the road, and they can be permanent.

Diving back into the story, we see that the lying and deceiving spirit speaks through the false prophets and Ahab runs off into battle. He ends up dead, while God spares Jehoshaphat. I am still puzzled that Jehoshaphat went with him, especially since he knew better. But this is simply proof to me that too many Christians are persuaded by performances. Sadly, these folks end up on battlefields where they do not belong.

I remember reading this story and meditating, looking for myself in the narrative. There is such a contrast between Ahab and Micaiah. Ahab was a man who led from a place of weakness. Any leader who intentionally surrounds himself with only puppets and performers is weak. The need to be affirmed, applauded, and acclaimed are not desires that should be found in a leader over God's children. Unfortunately, I've found that this happens way too often in our churches.

But then there's Micaiah, a man who was not persuaded—not by four hundred false prophets, not by a messenger sent by the king, not by the horns of iron, and not even by the threats of a king or threats to his life. He stayed steadfast. He was a man of unwavering commitment, a man of faith who knew who he was—God's man. Micah would remain true to himself and God.

Ahab, the king of Israel and the king of God's people, was repeatedly confronted with truths pointing him toward God. But he was hell-bent on doing things his way, indirectly rebuking God by ignoring Him and surrounding himself with people who would perform for him. All his performers lied to him so he could keep up his performance of being a tough king. Who suffered in the end? Only King Ahab did—the others went their merry way, satisfied with their performance.

Remember, my friend, if you forget who you are—a child of the King, redeemed by Christ—you will feel and act like something you are not. It is akin to attempting to put a puzzle together without seeing the picture of the puzzle. You can work, work, work, but there is no vision in sight. Additionally, with no vision of the finished product, one never knows if there is a counterfeit piece amongst the puzzle pieces. When you know what you are working on and what you are working with, the puzzle comes together.

So often I have seen Christian men determined to surround themselves with only those who put a stamp of approval on their behavior so they can continue in their sin. But this is the path of Ahab, destined for calamity and destruction. I have followed that path before; I knew what crowd went along with what behavior. I knew where to find the false prophets who would tell me what I desired. I have also found myself doing this while in relationship with Christ—it has never worked out well.

When the old man wants to start acting out, I think of Joseph, Daniel, and Micaiah. I encourage you to read their stories. Their steadfastness and their unwillingness to conform to the moment or the leadership around them drives me to do the same. Find a Christian friend and confess the mask you might be wearing. You will find rest in not having to perform. I fought that battle for most of my life in my struggle to find value. But help arrived on September 6th. As life moved on from that day, I would discover my value and worth in simply being who God created me to be—no performances needed.

Performance on Steroids

Prison was a three-plus year study hall. As you have seen in other chapters, I grew tremendously in Christ during those years. But in addition to studying the scriptures, I also had to assess and come to terms with the damage and carnage I'd left behind. The drug business is a violent business. Dad never understood this truth. Somehow he had convinced himself that sitting at home while others were doing the work removed him from any culpability. In his mind, he was just the finance guy, lulled into a blindness that hid his eyes from the pain and destruction of our actions.

Dad struggled with his prison sentence often. He always claimed he was "a nonviolent felon." He knew people who had been convicted of murder who received lesser sentences than him, and it drove him nuts. While our part of the drug operation was mostly drama-free, the destruction, damage, and violence that was waged upon our families and city was horrific. He never accepted that analysis.

For me it was different. I had accepted the depravity of my sin before God and had confessed (endlessly) all I could recall. And even then, I knew I still had to deal with my behavior. It would be with the help of the Lord, a great Christian psychologist, a counselor, and a Christian counselor at the Federal Prison Camp in Cumberland, MD, where I came to terms with the depravity of our actions.

A Green Pasture

God used His word and those three men for nine months, five days a week, 4–6 hours a day to pick apart the lives of myself and twenty-seven other men. I was part of a program that, if completed successfully, would grant a one-year reduction in time served and a six-month reduction of time in a halfway house, which equated to eighteen months out of prison early. It was in that program where God used these men to strip me bare and reveal my heart.

I remember standing in front of that group one day and having my heart wrecked. It was there that my counselor asked what I thought about someone selling drugs to my children. It was there that my counselor, Mr. Beal, asked me, "So, Hardy, is your life more valuable than others?" It was in that class where my counselor asked me, "What punishment do you think you deserve?" The amount of money and cocaine involved could have brought a 25-year sentence.

There are no words to describe the anguish in my heart and soul. I knew I had transgressed against God, but it became clear that I had also transgressed against hundreds of people. There was no satisfactory answer to what punishment I deserved. I could only believe that I had received what God had allowed. God and the judge had been merciful. The judge set aside the judgment that I deserved, just as God had set aside His judgment on those who confess Christ as Lord and Savior.

It is important to note that God set aside the judgment that the believer deserved, but God did not set aside the penalty that sin required. The believer did not receive grace and mercy at the expense of God's judgment. Rather than enacting His judgment on the sinner, it was applied to Christ. This is where the Christian faith really sets itself apart from all others; God did not throw away judgment in view of mercy, but instead placed His judgment on Christ.

How ironic that I, a guilty man, had received mercy because of a judge setting aside full judgment, while Christ, an innocent man, received no mercy so I would have the opportunity to not be judged by God.

Mr. Beal, my prison counselor, reminded me of Psalm 51 not long after that rough day in front of the class. I sat in his office with a friend as we read these words: *"Restore to me the joy of Your salvation, And sustain me with a willing spirit. Then I will teach wrongdoers Your ways, and sinners will be converted to You."* (verses 12–13) I made up my mind that day, and all the days following, that I would rejoice in my divine forgiveness and restoration. I would trust in God for the strength to persevere through good times and the worst of times. I vowed to accept the consequences of my earthly actions with no pushing back. I would take my life and do my best to allow Christ to use me to influence others for Him.

It was also there where God revealed that much of my life had consisted of those one-man shows strung together. So often I had gone against my conscience, but I was too pleased with putting on a performance. But a conscience void of Christ is a slippery slope; things usually slide to the bottom. It was during those nine months when I was first introduced to the word "value." Sure, I had heard the word before, but never in reference to myself. I had learned quickly of God's love, mercy, grace, and forgiveness, but I wavered in my value. I knew God loved me, but I still felt unworthy.

Many new Christians struggle after their conversion with continued thoughts of their previous sin, and I was no different. How was I to accept the love of God and the value He placed on my life while the consequences of my actions were so glaring? I knew God loved me, but what if everyone else disliked me?

Remember those "green pastures" from Psalm 23? Well, Cumberland Prison became one for me. It was a place where God had my attention.

The Tin Man and the Felon

Whenever I hear a news story about some individual who has committed an unspeakable act, I always think the same thought: at one time, that person was a child. That person was once a baby, a toddler, a child who did nothing more than dream about what all kids dream about; being a kid. And I have to wonder—what happened between the baby and the crime?

I will not claim to have all the answers on the subject. It is broad, and there are numerous experts who will tell you of the failure of the home, politicians, society, schools, and such. I will not speak to that, but I can speak to me.

Recently I was browsing through some old photo albums from my mom. I found all these pictures of a child at a petting zoo, on a fishing boat, blowing out candles on a cake, or dressed as a tin man. In each picture, I tried to imagine that kid—me—thinking about a life of crime, doing drugs, or selling cocaine with my dad. I never envisioned myself wearing the hat of the so-called tough guy, but it happened. I never dreamed of those things as a kid. In fact, I never got in much trouble as a kid, other than the time I gave my sister a whack. (She then fake cried so I would get into trouble—a funny memory now.)

So what happened in my life between those pictures and the drug addictions and prison? Why did I venture farther than others in my sins? At first glance, it might seem to be a combination of a lack of fear and stupidity. But that is too easy of an answer, for fearful and smart people still miss the Promised Land. So what is it that turned the Tin Man into a two-time felon?

Abundance

Here is the simple answer: I never knew who I was. I never knew that life had a value that was unmovable, unchanging, and eternal, and that it was there for me. Jesus beautifully stated in John 10:10, *"The thief comes only to steal and kill and destroy; I came so that they would have life and have it abundantly."*

I had lived as the thief, trying to enter a fullness and a fake Promised Land that was limited at best. Then, as I grew in awareness of God, Christ, and the Bible, I continued the life of thievery, seeking to enter God's fullness by some other way than through Christ. But Jesus did not turn His back. He sent Len to knock on my door, and four years later he was still there praying with me and speaking of the Promised Land in my driveway. How overwhelmed I felt when first discovering that Christ had come for people like me. He came to provide abundance. From that first day with Len until now, I continue to grow in my awareness of His abundance. There is no depletion in His provisions.

My prison counselor shared this verse with me one afternoon in his office, and it has continued to bring me comfort. James 4:8 says, *"Come close to God and He will come close to you. Cleanse your hands, you sinners; and purify your hearts, you double-minded."* The word double-minded refers to one who is trying to keep one foot in the world and one foot with God. Someone who is wearing a mask—putting on a performance. James is writing this message to believers. Through him, God is calling an end to performance and teeter-totter Christianity. It is not supposed to be a balancing act.

Over the years, I have met so many men who are still trying to put on a performance. As a men's ministry leader, I have spoken to dozens and dozens of men who feel inadequate with their identity. So often, broken people are still trying to perform for a parent who is no longer on this earth. They are still trying to be the person their parents wanted them to be instead of accepting themselves as divinely created, purposed, and positioned by God. Too many people are imprisoned by memories of the past, shaped by someone else's voice and actions, still determined to perform for the dead into their 80's and 90's.

It is due time that the Christian lives for Christ. The apostle Paul knew what it meant to live when he said, *"For to me, to live is Christ, and to die is gain."* (Philippians 1:21). Paul knew that life was not an act or performance. I have learned that my life presents a vessel by which Christ can live His life. We lend Him our voice and mouth.

Christ did not do performances. The cross was one act. It will never happen again, as the writer of Hebrews reminds us, *"but He, having offered one sacrifice for sins for all time, SAT DOWN AT THE RIGHT HAND OF GOD."* (Hebrews 10:12).

In prison, I learned that all people are shaped and molded by something or someone. The performance is most often that of a life that emulates and complements the shaper. As parents, we smile when we see our kids practice something wholesome that we taught them. But other times, we grimace at what they've picked up from us.

So as we influence our kids, grandkids, and others in our lives, the goal is to shape them in a way that the person is not conditioned to perform to find personal value. Bottom line, whether the kid rides the bench or plays every down, they should feel just as valuable.

Whether you agree or disagree with someone's political opinion, you are just as valuable. Whether you attend *this* church or *that* church, you are just as valuable. God does not have a list of favorites amongst His children.

My Lack of Identity

It is hard to persevere when one is fighting to find fulfillment. The pressures of life always pushed me into another practice that was not healthy or Godly. Tough times moved me like that old pinball, bouncing and ricocheting around and never resting. It was the entrance into the Promised Land and the promises of scripture that provided endurance through tribulations.

If you pick up my Bible and turn to 2 Corinthians 4:17, you will see the word *WOW* written in the margin. I have continually traced over it, never wanting it to fade. I even have the words, "Are you kidding me?" written next to the verse. Here is what it says: *"For our momentary, light affliction is producing for us an eternal weight of glory far beyond all comparison."*

Amazing. It's even more amazing when you realize that the Apostle Paul states in 2 Corinthians 11:26–28, "I have been *on frequent journeys, in dangers from rivers, dangers from robbers, dangers from my countrymen, dangers from the Gentiles, dangers in the city, dangers in the wilderness, dangers at sea, dangers among false brothers; I have been in labor and hardship, through many sleepless nights, in hunger and thirst, often without food, in cold and exposure. Apart from such external things, there is the daily pressure on me of concern for all the churches."*

Read that again and remember that Paul considered this a "light affliction." When you know who you are, you can have this attitude about whatever you are facing.

Learning and Growing

When I was walking out of the door of prison, the last thing my two wonderful counselors told me was this: "Hey, Hardy. Be wise, be God-focused, for the old crowd will roll out the red carpet for you, ready to make you a rock star again."

My first thought? *No way I would ever make that mistake.* I had learned during those prison years, especially the last months, that it was okay for me to be me—God's child. No more performances were needed, nor did I need to surround myself with performers.

But you know what? Just like prophets, my counselors were correct. I had been out of prison for about seven months when I received a call from an unlisted number. I answered, and I immediately recognized the voice. It was a voice from my past—a man who had sold us kilos. After small talk, he asked me if I was interested in getting back in the business.

Here was my answer: "Well, you know, I just got out of prison, and I am not doing that anymore. So, no thanks."

He replied, "Okay, well, I will check-in from time to time."

Did you catch how pitiful of a statement I made? Well, I didn't at first, but I was quickly made aware of it when I went to see a mentor of mine.

Pastor Wayne operated a huge prison and street ministry. When I was visiting him, I told Pastor Wayne what had happened. He asked me what I said to the guy, and when I told him, he sure took me to the woodshed.

"What kind of answer is that?" he asked sternly, yet lovingly. "What strength do you have to continue to tell him no when he calls back?"

I did my best to tell him of my bravado and new life. But he did not have any of it.

"Are you embarrassed to be a follower of Christ?"

"No sir."

"Well it seems to me you were living closer to the old Mike than the new Mike."

His wife, Mama Ann, looked at me and said, "Mike, Jesus went to the cross for you, so that you could live with Him and for Him."

They were correct. I had not mentioned my faith; I purposely left it out. I could not believe it—seven years as a believer and I faltered. And even worse, it was to someone over a phone. However, I did not stay down. I asked Pastor Wayne what he suggested. Together, we rehearsed my response for the next time my old acquaintance would call. We even practiced different scenarios. Pastor Wayne was reminding me who I was in Christ.

Guess what? My old drug partner called again, trying again to roll out the red carpet for me. I was ready this time.

"I am sorry. I did not mention this the last time you called, but I am a Christian now. I have given my life to Christ, and I am living for Him now, so no, I cannot do those things anymore."

I will not print the remark I heard in return, but after a few more pleasantries, I hung up. Pastor Wayne had predicted that one of two things would happen: one, he would ask about how to become a Christian, or two, he would leave me alone. My old friend chose number two. At first, I felt so pitiful. I had failed the test. But I used that moment as a teaching moment, once again reminding you and me that we must be intentional about serving Christ.

Here is what I often tell my kids, even though they are older, "As a saved follower of Jesus Christ, when you find that your conscience is pushing back against your present actions, you better stop." I usually add, "You may not be quite sure about what to do next, but stop for a moment and ask

God to make things clear." I have learned to trust in that inner voice, the voice of Christ's whisper in my heart. After that first phone call, I did not feel right about my weak answer; I felt convicted, but I did not react. I thank the Lord for His perseverance with me. His continued presence has enabled me to become a better listener ... and responder.

Escape to the Promised Land

It was in the Promised Land where I found deliverance and fullness. It is there where I find my value and worth. Have I made mistakes? Yes, big ones. But God did not boot me out or deny me reentry to His land of infinite goodness. There is no performance needed to please our Lord, only a heart that has repented and received Him as Lord and Savior. Sure, obedience is required, but not for His benefit but for ours. I have never regretted obedience, but I sure have huge regrets about disobedience. I found fullness and abundance in the Promised Land, and you will also. God expounds on this fullness in Deuteronomy 8, when He reminds the Israelite nation that they were not to forget His provisions and protection in the wilderness. But also, He describes what they would find in the Promised Land, saying,

*"For the Lord your God is bringing you into a good land, a land of streams of water, of fountains and springs, flowing out in valleys and hills; a land of wheat and barley, of vines, fig trees, and pomegranates, a land of olive oil and honey; a land where you will eat food without shortage, **in which you will not lack anything;** a land whose stones are iron, and out of whose hills you can dig copper. **When you have eaten and are satisfied,** you shall bless the Lord your God for the good land which He has given you."* (Deuteronomy 8:7–10, emphasis mine).

How beautiful, how assuring, how comforting, and how powerful. As God says, "You will not lack anything." (verse 9). I have never found "something" that could supplant the "anything" of that verse. Not even chocolate pie trumps the abundance of the Promised Land.

Reflection Questions

1. In what area of your life have you practiced performance?

2. As a follower of Christ, was your performance in contradiction with your conscience?

3. Is there someone in your life for whom you are still performing?

4. Who are you? Find ten Bible verses that define how God sees you. Here is a good start to your list.

   • You are God's child. *"But as many as received Him, to them He gave the right to become children of God, to those who believe in His name."* John 1:12

   • You are a friend of God. *"No longer do I call you slaves, for the slave does not know what his master is doing; but I have called you friends ... "* John 15:15a

   • You are free, for Jesus has given you a real, non-counterfeit freedom. *"So if the Son sets you free, you really will be free."* John 8:36

5. Do you need people to agree with you or tell you the truth? Be honest.

6. What does your peer group look like? Are they Godly people with Godly counsel?

7. Is it necessary to always receive Godly counsel? At home? Regarding morals? At work? With financial advice?

8. Has anyone tried to roll out the red carpet for you? How did you manage the situation?

9. How would you define the Promised Land?

10. What moment or moments in your life were watershed moments in your life with Christ? Have you thought about writing these down for your family or kids to have and cherish?

9

WHERE THE PROMISED LAND
IS NOT FOUND—PEOPLE

People = Relationships

Texas Sheet Cake is my favorite dessert. I know I already
shared about my "chocolate pie," but hey, I love chocolate.

For as long as Mom was making my birthday cakes, this is
the one she made every year—a full-sized Texas Sheet Cake.
Whenever she finished baking the cake, she would give me

one beater covered in icing, and she would take the other. There was always a special bond between us when making that sheet cake.

So our last pie-in-the-sky isn't so much a pie, but rather the Texas Sheet Cake that we share with the people in our lives. People become a pie-in-the-sky when we pursue relationships to find value and acceptance. As you no doubt can guess, it is the last in our list because it is the common thread that runs through all of the other areas we've discussed.

Relationships without Christ

I always enjoyed traveling with my dad. It did not seem to matter where we traveled; he knew someone who could get us tickets, get us seated, get us a room—just flat out get anything. He knew people who could make things happen. To this day I still do not understand some of the strings he was able to pull. I was especially awed by his connections in New York. On more than one occasion, a phone number on a piece of paper mysteriously produced play tickets and dinner reservations, all delivered to the hotel desk. Dad had relationships in New York that allowed the limo to pull to the front door of the Palladium and Limelight, and entrance was granted immediately, regardless of the hundreds of people standing in line. Great food and comped dinners at some of New York's best hidden restaurants—it was almost like visiting fantasy island on some trips with my dad.

I was enthralled by the idea that the right relationships could provide anything one wanted. The right relationship always got a table at one of Atlanta or New York's best steakhouses, no matter how busy they were. Of course, honest folks practice these things legitimately all the time. But what it was doing to my heart was devastating. I had watched

The Godfather too many times, and I was hooked. There just seemed to be a strength that came with being connected to the right people—a strength that seemed to add value to who I was.

The right relationships were necessary during the drug years because they provided safety and security. In that business, if you cannot protect yourself and your investment, you will not last long. I had lived in South Florida during the drug years, and on more than one occasion I spent time with celebrities. My reputation, cash, and cocaine opened that door. I remember thinking at the time, *Oh, how cool am I?* Only now do I see I was an idiot—a poster child for insecurity. Relationships with others only existed to add value to myself, both externally and internally.

There is nothing inherently wrong with feeling the joy and specialness that exude from personal relationships. We have been created to live in relationships. Loneliness can be devastating—we need relationships to live a healthy Christian life. But no relationship, other than one with Christ, adds intrinsic value to your life in God's eyes. But at the time, the "right relationships" we engaged in were reciprocal relationships. We got what we wanted, and they got what they wanted—money and things.

During those years my dad was generous, and I was generous. In truth, we gave away thousands of dollars to all sorts of people. We enjoyed great relations with all those folks. But you know what? When we went to prison, we never saw those folks again. Those relationships vanished.

Relationships built on sand crumble when the storms of life appear. Remember when Jesus asked Peter in Matthew 16:13, *"Who do people say that the Son of Man is?"* Peter responded by saying, *"You are the Christ, the Son of the living God."* (verse 15). Christ replied, *"'Blessed are you, Simon*

Barjona, because flesh and blood did not reveal this to you, but My Father who is in heaven. And I also say to you that you are Peter, and upon this rock I will build My church; and the gates of Hades will not overpower it."' (verse 17–18). Christ would build His church on the truth of what Peter had stated—a Church built on a rock, built through relationships with God only through Jesus Christ.

But back when I was visiting my dad in the Atlanta Penitentiary, he said to me, "It seems that most all my friends were made of straw—they have blown away in the wind." These were relationships built on sand. It was true that people had seemingly vanished. But I believe many people were caught off guard when he was arrested, and Dad himself was much of the reason as well. He was bitter, and he was bitter at everyone. However, in the end, it was the Christian folks he knew that reached out to him, and many continued to do so for more than twenty-two years.

Now I know that in the next few weeks, I will call up Tim at one of my favorite restaurants and ask him to hold a table for me. He's a Christian, and he runs the place like one. But this is a very different kind of "calling in" than my dad did years ago. Tim is a great friend, but my relationship with him does not define my worth. That relationship does not add any more value to my being in God's eyes. But true friendship adds immeasurable value to my life experience.

Differences

There is joy in the differences between us. Let's face it, without uniqueness in our relationships, life becomes boring. Who wants only people who are like-minded, with the same career, hobbies, and opinions as their peer group? I certainly do not—that would get boring and monotonous. I have great friends who enjoy sports, and others who hate sports. Some love going to the beach, while others cannot stand the sand. Some love talking politics, and some cringe at the conversation. I have friends who get up at 5 AM, and friends who sleep until mid-morning. Bottom line, I am surrounded and blessed with a variety of wonderful friends, each unique and valuable in God's eyes. My love for them is based on the truth of Christ's love for me, my love for Him, and the love Christ has commanded His followers to demonstrate towards others. Christ simply brings people together.

Because the topic of relationships is the Texas Sheet Cake pie-in-the-sky, I recently did a Google search for "chocolate cake recipe." It resulted in 345 million options for chocolate junkies. In comparison, the approximate population of the United States as of May 2023 was about 334 million. Theoretically, there seems to be at least one chocolate cake for each person in the country. One unique cake for each unique individual.

Relationships operate in a similar fashion, in that each person brings a somewhat different flavor—or recipe, you might say—to each relationship. We not only look different, but we operate differently. We may naturally take on similar mannerisms and character when with our closest friends, for as it is said, "Birds of a feather flock together." But even then, each connection is a tad bit different.

So why are we different? Well, simply stated, God creates each human differently. Each person is a unique design by God, to God, and for God. Psalm 139:16a says beautifully, *"Your eyes have seen my unformed substance; And in Your book were written All the days that were ordained for me."* King David knew that God knew him from his time as a fetus until his last day. Jeremiah wrote, *"Before I formed you in the womb I knew you."* (Jeremiah 1:5a). Not only has God created each living soul, but scripture also states He knew each of us before we were even in the womb.

This biblical truth has become even more apparent and thrilling thanks to the discovery of the double helix structure of our DNA back in 1953. Because of that discovery, we now know that each person is similar in that we share 99.9 percent of the same DNA. But that remaining 0.1 percent creates a uniqueness for each human.

Common Denominator

Though we are each created uniquely and differ in our DNA and personalities, man shares the same creator, and each of us was created in God's image. Genesis 1:27 records, *"So God created man in His own image, in the image of God He created him; male and female He created them."* Sure, one can see God's handiwork in all His creation, but the only place to see His image is to look at mankind. God poured His wisdom and divine intellect into all of His creation, and divinely designed it all with the instinct to care for itself. But only humans possess the image of God.

The notion of "image" can be confusing, so allow me to explain a little. I am not so ridiculous as to equate God to my body size and looks. But I am His image in the characteristics and attributes that we share through Christ. John MacArthur states, "Man is a living being capable of embodying God's communicable attributes," *(The MacArthur Study Bible).*[16]

We were created with the ability to communicate with God. Communication presupposes a relationship. Further, man is comprised of mind, spirit, and soul, which also applies to Jesus Christ. For when Christ appeared as the sinless incarnate son of God, He also appeared as a man, possessing a mind, spirit, and soul.

Scripture also reveals that God's design was for His followers to be conformed to the image of His Son. We see this in Romans 8:29a: *"For those whom He foreknew, He also predestined* to become *conformed to the image of His Son."* We see that God's goal for His children is simply that we become like Christ. This begins with relationship, as a personal relationship with Jesus Christ provides the only access to God. Even more wonderful, we see that those who know Christ as Lord and Savior can love God like Christ, can be obedient like Christ, and can enjoy relationships as Christ modeled. We know this is true and possible because of Matthew 22:37–39, where it states, *"YOU SHALL LOVE THE LORD YOUR GOD WITH ALL YOUR HEART AND WITH ALL YOUR SOUL AND WITH ALL YOUR MIND." This is the great and foremost commandment. The second is like it, "You shall love your neighbor as yourself,"* (emphasis mine).

Remember, God does not issue commands that are not possible to follow. That statement is a biblical truth that has helped transform my life. As I wanted so desperately to put my life together, it was consistent encouragement to learn that God's commands were not tests of our abilities, but rather tests of our obedience. Thus when the command to love thy neighbor is given, we are not left helpless or asked to search for the neighbor that is capable of being loved—we simply are equipped to love whomever God puts in front of us.

Fallen Nature

What makes this difficult is that the nature of fallen man is to corrupt that which God intended for good. Apart from the guiding influence of Christ and His Holy Spirit, man is left to his own devices and methods. Yes, humans can be loving, creative, entertaining, personable, and friendly, but absent of a relationship with Christ, man is left to his own self-righteousness.

Look at Luke 18:9. *"Now He also told this parable to some people who trusted in themselves that they were righteous, and viewed others with contempt."* Jesus then went on to tell a parable about a Pharisee and a tax collector going to the temple to pray. The Pharisee thanked God that he was not a sinner like the tax collector. But the tax collector prayed for mercy (Luke 18:10–14). It's a powerful comparison of the self-righteous and the humble.

Did you catch how Christ identified His listening audience? They were recognizable as the ones who trusted in themselves and had contempt for others. In other words, self-righteous. This is the attitude of a Pharisee: one who makes his own laws and rules as he goes along, then creates a god that will put a stamp of approval on those rules. He manages all relationships by his own standard.

These were the kind of relationships I enjoyed many years ago. Yes, I have had lots of friends, but until Christ came into my life, I was always the most important one in the relationship. I was a true Pharisee—everything went according to my rules. But I discovered a truth in the Promised Land: a Christian should never emulate a Pharisee. We simply cannot make up the rules as we go along. We belong to Christ; it is His rule book we follow.

I do recognize that believers have issues. Christians often disagree, divorce, fight, argue, and have plenty of sin problems. We know that on any given day, a Christian who takes His mind and heart off Christ is capable of any behavior. But please remember that a Christian has a choice to sin or not to sin, to love as Christ or not to love; a person void of Christ has no choice.

Sad Observations

In my early years as a Christian, I was shocked at the different cliques that had formed within the local church body. I thought the church, though filled with diverse personalities, would operate on a level much different from the world. But sadly, this has become standard procedure for most churches. Of course, any time more than one person is involved, different personalities can clash, but I surely thought a relationship with Christ would rule the day and be the standard for relationships within the body. But to my consternation, this has not been true.

It seems that many Christians love to quote "Love thy neighbor as thyself," (Matthew 22:39b, KJV) more than they love to fulfill that command. It seems to be too easy for Christians to dismiss other Christians, and do so in the name of Jesus. It is no wonder the outside world looks at the Church and sees themselves. Just imagine if you were outside the church, outside of a relationship with Christ, and your view of the church looked just like the world in which you were living. Why would you think you needed the church?

When people tell me of the attitudes that they have encountered at churches, I tell them, "I get it." However, I do not leave it there. I remind them that most folks visit a second McDonald's after one bad experience—or visit a second doctor, a second lawyer, et cetera. I try to encourage them to look at Christ and His Words rather than the people. But people are the problem—people and a watered-down gospel.

The church is the last place where cliques and inner circles should exist, as it eventually causes detriment to others. Yes, people develop deeper relationships and best friends are made, but these should never be exercised to the harm of others. No one in God's church should ever feel less valuable than someone else. However, I am afraid that the value of relationships in making disciples and growing the Church has been dismissed in lieu of music, performances, events, and watered-down preaching. Of course, this is not true everywhere, but it is becoming a trend. And it shows; small groups are dwindling, and church attendance is declining across all Christian groups.

This is devastating news, as the power and influence of relationships are being set aside. We each would like to believe that our church is a place of Christlike hospitality where the Spirit within the body is conducive to developing great relationships. However, experience teaches that 90 minutes sitting in the pew, listening to preaching, and singing do not require a personal relationship with anyone, including the Lord. (Reread Matthew 7:13 and 21—there are many in the Church who are not true believers in Christ.)

Our early church fathers were convinced that sharing the gospel and communicating with people could bring people to Christ. The book of Acts reveals a growing church because, " ... *the word of God kept on spreading; and the number of disciples continued to increase greatly in Jerusalem ...* " (Acts 6:7 a). The plan? Preach and teach the Gospel and disciple people.

My good friend Pastor Fred heads a small ministry called "Dynamic Small Groups." It is designed to help churches grow through discipleship, primarily through growing the small groups that used to be so prevalent in all denominations. Here is a quote from his website, dynamicsmallgroups.org:

> From the Old Testament to the New Testament small groups are used in very significant ways. Small Groups

have always been part of God's plan to develop and grow believers. In modern times from Sunday School to the contemporary Small Group movement the churches that embraced small groups in a significant way experienced the most growth in evangelism and discipleship. Small Groups should be a fundamental strategy for every church that seeks to be a Biblically complete church.[17]

You know what Pastor Fred is saying? Churches grow through relationships.

Sadly though, this is becoming a dinosaur. The goal for many ministers today is to reach a certain total in attendance. "How fast can we get from 450 to 2000 in attendance," is the goal. I hear this rhetoric and I cringe, as the conversation never centers around Christ or souls. I believe the focus on attendance numbers is a sign of the worldly church. Once again, Christ said that *"the way is broad that leads to destruction, and there are **many** who enter through it."* (Matthew 7:13b, emphasis mine). Whenever man seeks center stage, sooner or later Christ is left in the wings.

Now, I am not against growth and counting people, for living entities grow and a living church is to grow and further good. Business sense does often apply even in churches. But a number focus leaves so many on the doorsteps of Hell. Proverbs 27:17 says that iron sharpens iron. This only happens when iron touches iron—we need to get close enough to each other to have any sort of relationship.

The best avenue to create this atmosphere is through communicating and interacting with one another. Pastor Fred might be called a dinosaur by some, but he is spot-on in his analysis of church growth. The church is being led astray by its attraction to its own talent. Music, choir specials, and events can present the gospel pretty well. But they are relatively easy

as compared to relationships. It is relationships that take
time, love, and perseverance—but relationships pay off with
eternal rewards.

The Neighbors

When it comes to relationships, scripture reveals that authentic Christlike faith is to seek healing, not wounding.
Reread the parable of the good Samaritan in Luke 10:25-37.

In the story, Jesus describes a scene of a man being attacked
by robbers along the road. The man is stripped, beaten, and
left for dead. Along walks a priest—but he passes by on the
other side of the road. Then comes a Levite, who does the
same. Finally a Samaritan appears—an outcast to Jews. But
despite their cultural boundaries, the Samaritan bandages
the man's wounds, puts him on his donkey, and brings him
to an inn to take care of him.

Two strangers had an encounter; one was in great need,
while the other was hated and despised by the community.
But that did not deter the outcast's heart, and compassion
prevailed—the Samaritan went the extra mile and shared the
love of Christ. Listen to Jesus speak as He closes the parable,
speaking to His followers (which includes you and me), " ...
'Go and do the same.'" (verse 37).

In his story Christ clearly reveals the magnitude by which a
person should love others. The two people who should have
known the love of God—the priest and the Levite—are portrayed as self-righteous, ignoring the hurting man. But the
Samaritan, a hated person, went the extra mile and shared
the love of Christ. Clearly the priest and Levite did not have a
love for God as defined in Deuteronomy 6:4-5, for a love for
God would be manifested in a love for one's fellow man.

Here is the point Jesus was getting at in his message—if

you love God as you should, then you will love people as you should, in spite of whatever. Sadly, for our culture on the whole, too much emphasis is placed on the worthiness of the one to be loved rather than the love of the one who is commanded to love his brother.

There will be no bragging points in heaven for not loving someone.

Are you catching the theme here? "'[Love] your neighbor as yourself,'" and, "'Go and do the same.'" (Luke 10:26, 37). Remember, God does not command that which cannot be lived out.

When it comes to the story of the Good Samaritan, I am afraid that many people have forgotten the identity of their neighbor. Who is our neighbor? Who are we to love? How about the next person you run into—any and everybody you can share the gospel message with, whether through word or action?

Now this is not a universal love that ignores sin. There should be a deep hatred of the sin, and a heartfelt sorrow for the one who is plagued by the disease of sin. But we must also have a prayerful compassion for the sinner. And yes, sometimes this means we separate ourselves from others physically, but not spiritually. Remember, love is never to negate God's call to holiness.

We must learn how to separate the sin from the sinner. From speaking and mentoring at the local mission over the years, I have found that it is too easy to give up on folks because of their heinous actions and behaviors. I have seen rock bottom redefined numerous times. But I have learned that I cannot quit praying for these folks, for I have seen some of the most amazing recoveries and turn-arounds all in the name of Jesus.

If you give up praying for someone, you will not be ready

to love them or help them when they do turn around. And since we are not God and know not who will or will not turn, we are mandated to pray for each.

Every turn-around and miracle that I have seen take place has involved relationships—first with Christ and then other believers. If we can persevere for the non-believer, how much more should we persevere for each other? I am all for Church discipline as the Bible has outlined. The apostle Paul, when dealing with a sexual sin in the Corinthian Church, wrote after the individual had been excommunicated for a season, *"Sufficient for such a person is this punishment which was imposed by the majority, so that on the other hand, you should rather forgive and comfort him, otherwise such a person might be overwhelmed by excessive sorrow. Therefore, I urge you to reaffirm your love for him."* (2 Corinthians 2:6-8). Repentance is assumed and implied. But there comes a point when relationships need to prevail.

Listen, too many stand-alone Christians are picked off by Satan. We love people not because we are checking off a box on a list or getting our holy card punched, but rather because we love Christ and His words. We just do not have the internal wiring to be Christlike unless we have Christ in our hearts.

A Rocky Start

Most everyone who arrives in prison for the first time is nervous. Guys may act big, bad, and bold upon arrival, but they are deeply anxious and nervous. I know this because for six months, I worked under the Chaplain in Petersburg. A new guy in prison usually stops by the Chaplain's office to inquire about church services, and he is usually at the first church service that is available to him. However, allow a month or so to go by, and those that have taken off like a rocket end up dropping like a rock, never to be seen in church again.

When I first arrived at prison, I was also nervous. My mind was working overtime, thinking through all of the prison scenes I'd seen in the movies. I did not know what to expect. But I knew Christ was in me and with me.

The first days were spent in orientation. I was learning where things were and learning the rules—written and unwritten. It was easy to pick up the chow hall times, the shower rules, dress rules, visiting regulations, and such. Those rules were mostly static; they never changed. However, it was the unwritten rules—the rules of what you do and don't do amongst the other inmates—where there was a learning curve.

I was green and had only received one piece of advice from my dad, who was in a tough, dangerous prison in Atlanta: "Do not fight over the phone, do not gamble, mind your own business."

I learned the truth about the phone quickly. In prison, there is only one phone for about 150 guys. There were about three hundred inmates, so we had two phones. Phone calls are limited to fifteen minutes, and an inmate can only access his phone account through a pin number once every ninety minutes. Additionally, inmates are limited to 300 minutes of phone time a month. As you can imagine, the phone is busy nonstop.

Well, on my first day of being able to use the phone, I walked by and saw that no one was on the phone at the moment. So I picked up the phone to start my call. Suddenly, another inmate snatched the phone out of my hand and told me in colorful language to back off. I walked away, confused, until an inmate I'd met in church service, Harold, graciously explained the system to me.

The phone is in constant use, but there is no visible line waiting to use the phone. Instead there is an invisible line that forms, where each inmate is responsible for knowing who is ahead of him and who is after him in line. So if I wanted to use the phone, I would yell out, "Who is last in line for the phone?" and hope that somebody would speak up. That put me last in line until someone came along and asked me to put them in the phone line. When finished with my call, I would holler that I was done, and the next guy got his turn. It was normal to wait hours before you got your phone call.

After learning the rules, I asked around and was told that JB was last in line. So off I went to go find this JB and tell him that I was now last in line. I asked around and learned that his cubicle was on the third floor. So off I went, walking up the range in front of the cubicles, hollering for JB. That was when I suddenly found myself face-to-face with a 6'5" Muslim black guy. (I mention his race for a reason, as you'll see later on.) Let me tell you, he got my attention—JB had been in prison for twenty years, and in no uncertain words, he let me know I was never to speak his name again, come near his cubicle again, or even look at him again. I apologized and walked away, waiting for someone else to grab the spot behind JB before getting in line myself.

I was told later that I showed weakness by apologizing, but I was determined to live for Christ. As I walked away from JB, Harold called me over.

"Mike, you'll meet lots of people who might not care for you here," he told me. "Some people won't like you because of the color of your skin. But your focus should be on your personal walk with Christ." Harold modeled Christ everywhere he went in that prison. Christ has His faithful followers everywhere, as I have learned. I thank Jesus for sending him my way. I wished he had showed up five minutes earlier, but years later, I found out why he did not.

But for the time being, I knew how to use the phone and to stay away from JB and his crowd. I never spoke to him again for two years. There were a few times when I was in the Chapel vicinity when the Muslims were finishing their worship service, but when JB crossed my path, I would just smile, look straight ahead, and pray inwardly.

Living Through Laundry

During those first weeks (while avoiding getting in JB's way), I started to get the hang of prison routines. One of those routines was doing laundry.

In prison, there are a couple of options for doing laundry. An inmate can turn in a mesh bag filled with his dirty laundry once a week to have it washed for him. The other option is to use the laundry room, where he can do laundry himself in the provided washers and dryers for a cost.

I decided to do my own laundry, so I brought my clothes down to the laundry room, got the load started in the washer, and sat at a large table to read my Bible alone. Suddenly I heard a loud, sandpaper-throated voice bellowing from down the hallway. The voice proceeded to engage in some back-and-forth with another inmate about a foul called in a basketball game. Though I had only been in the prison for two weeks or so, I knew the voice.

The voice belonged to Wash, otherwise known as "The Commissioner." Everyone knew Wash. He had been in prison for twenty years and had served time in some of the toughest prisons in America. He was only about 5'10", but his width was massive and his strength was phenomenal. I had seen him at the outdoor weights at the prison several times, and he was one of the strongest guys by far. He was also the inmate who oversaw all of the inmate sporting events—volleyball, basketball, baseball, and football. He was an umpire or referee in almost every game. He had the respect of everyone, including the staff. He was completely unbothered by anything anyone said or did.

So when Wash marched into the laundry room, I was a bit nervous. I was not sure why, other than being unsure what to expect. He looked at me and said nothing. So I sat quietly and kept reading and journaling.

Wash took his clothes out of one of the dryers and headed toward the table where I was sitting, so I got up and moved to a corner seat against the wall. I watched him covertly—he had taken three dryers' worth of clothes out of the dryer and dumped them onto the table. As I watched, I suddenly felt my heart tell me to speak to him. I pushed back with my best intellect, but my heart would not stop—it was pounding.

So with a dry mouth, I asked, "Excuse me, but could you use some help?"

Wash turned and stared for a moment. "Why would you want to do that?"

"No real reason," I said. "It just looks like you could use some help, and I am just sitting here." I spoke cautiously. You must be careful about trying to buddy up with someone in prison. A person's intentions can be harmful, and even if not harmful, they can be misconstrued.

I joined him at the table and quietly began to fold his clothes. After a few minutes of silence, he spoke.

"Where are you from?"

I told him about Key West, and he told me a bit about where he was from. We finished up the laundry, he said a quick, "Thank you," and he walked out the door. Five seconds later, he stuck his head back in the laundry room.

"Do you lift weights?"

"Well," I said, "I have not done that in some years."

"Well, do you want to start?" he snapped back.

A hundred excuses ran through my head, trying to think of a way out. But before I could come up with something, my heart spoke for me. "Yes, I'd like to do that."

Wash smiled. "Okay. I'll see you tomorrow morning down at the weight pile at 7 a.m. Don't be late. And bring that white buddy of yours."

My mind flooded with thoughts as soon as he left the laundry room. *What the heck did I just commit to?* Who *did I just commit to?*

I went back to the dorm and told the one guy I'd been spending time with. He was thrilled. He exclaimed that it was "a great opportunity." So the next morning, we were at the weight pile ready to go.

That voice in my heart in the laundry room that day led me to the most beautiful unlikely relationship. I began to go to the weight pile each morning, five days a week. We began to talk and visit even away from the weight pile.

From those mornings at the weights, I learned about Wash, and he learned about me. He was black, and he had grown up poor on his dad's sharecropper pay. He had dropped out of school, and up until prison, he drove dump trucks and sold cocaine on the streets in the Washington D.C. area. He had a girlfriend; they had a child, and just a couple of years later he went to prison. He had been sentenced to twenty-six years for an infantile amount of cocaine compared to what we had smuggled. He was already in prison when I had left for college as a first-year student. There was no mercy in his courtroom. Further, when I met Wash, he had not had a visit or phone call in seventeen years. He had only received five letters in eighteen years.

I had grown up in privilege. I'd lived a completely different life from him. His world and my world were light years different—even our drug involvement was different. I hadn't even had a friend who was a different color since I was in eighth grade.

We listened to each other, and we shared our hearts. He taught me and I taught him—neither was wiser than the other, we just each had our own areas of "expertise." When I was taken away from the prison for those four months in Key West, I wondered often about Wash. I prayed for him and hoped we could continue our friendship.

I will never forget the day I arrived back in Petersburg. Wash saw me and hollered, "See you on the pile in the morning!" I was there the next day.

The next eighteen months saw our relationship blossom into the most beautiful of friendships. Others began to call us Salt and Pepper—little did they know I was trying to be another kind of salt. We spent all our time together when we were not working or sleeping ... or when I was in church. Wash simply would not come to church. "I have seen too many hypocrites," he would say. I would agree with him, and then remind him God was interested in him and his heart, not what others had done.

"I don't need the church," was his second response.

"Sure you do, or else God would not have given us the church," I would counter. Then he would grumble at me in that deep, rough voice.

My heart ached for Wash (as did my muscles). I prayed for him day and night. I would pray for him when we were together, silently interceding for him as I listened to him talk about whatever. There was a deep love I felt for this man—I knew it was Christ loving me, and loving Wash through me.

Oh how privileged we are to be part of the process of God loving someone.

Some of my friends from the church in Virginia Beach began to write to him, and many even got on his visiting list and began to visit him. He was amazed as he saw complete strangers demonstrate a real love and concern for him. He would come to learn that it was because of their relationship with Christ.

Finally, one day in my cubicle, Wash prayed and asked Christ into his heart. From that day on, he never missed church. He would sit in the front row with me. When we would stand and sing, we would often sway from side to side; occasionally I would bump into him, and I would almost hit the ground. This big, tough, strong guy had become a child in Christ.

My last six months in Petersburg were spent with him as we exercised our muscles and our hearts for Christ. I loved our Bible talks. He had heard his mother speak of these things, and he had loved gospel music, but he just did not want to let go of his heart. But the love of Christ prevailed.

I was there two years later when he walked out the door into freedom. He and I are still great friends today, and we will spend eternity together.

The Power of Relationship on Display

Wash and I weren't the only ones impacted by our friendship. Remember my story about JB? Well there's a bit more to the story about my relationship with him.

Remember how I was moved from Petersburg, VA to the Cumberland Maryland Federal Prison Camp? What I did not tell you about was my first day there at Cumberland. When an inmate is moved, he is clothed in regular civilian clothes and placed on a Greyhound bus. Yep, a Greyhound bus, as if you are being moved from Camp Custody to Camp Custody, with nothing other than the clothes on your back, your prison ID, and a paper bag with two apples and a pack of crackers. I arrived in Cumberland around noon, then caught a cab to the prison. I entered the prison, went through a thirty-minute orientation, got some clothes and work boots, and went off to the dorms to find my pod.

I entered my pod, which had two sets of bunk beds and one single bed. I was comforted when I ran into one of my friends from back in Virginia. I had forgotten he had been moved to Cumberland and was glad to know he would be my roommate for a few weeks. It was good to see a familiar face, and he quickly got me up to speed on the ins and outs of the place.

After about 45 minutes, my joy turned into panic. Suddenly, out of nowhere, in the entrance to our cubicle stood JB. I had no idea he was in Cumberland. I was frozen.

"Hardy, I heard you were here," he said.

"I just got here about an hour ago or so," I said as calmly as possible. I was so focused on trying to plan my next move that I hadn't even seen what he was holding in his hands. It was a shoe box.

JB spoke. "I know your property isn't here yet, so I got some things together for you." He walked up to me and handed me the shoebox. I reached my hands out to receive the box instinctually, so shocked and confused that I couldn't think clearly. I opened it up to find that it was filled with soap, shampoo, lotion, deodorant, toothpaste, some small snack items, and a few other things.

"I don't know what to say—"

"I know you're probably confused." JB said, cutting me off.

"I will pay you back," I blurted out.

He smiled and shook my hand as I cradled this most

unexpected gift under my arm. "You already paid me back,"
he said. "I have been watching you for two years. I saw what
you did with Wash. I and others appreciate what you did for
him. We know your Christianity was real."

Then he turned and walked away. This guy hated me two
years earlier, and now he was bringing me a gift. I set the box
down and told my friend I needed to use the restroom. I went
to a stall and cried.

JB would be released from Cumberland three months later.
I did not try to crowd him, but he spoke to me. He and the
others looked after me.

You know, JB never did become a Christian. He practiced
his faith, and I practiced mine. However, God taught me two
things about relationships. First, an authentic relationship
with Christ is attractive. When one lives out their faith, especially in loving others, people are simply drawn to that person and, hopefully and prayerfully, to their faith. My relationship with Wash was Christ-centered, and people had been
watching. Only God knows the other ripple effects that exist
because of Christ's work in our lives. Secondly, a relationship
with Christ can cause enemies to become friends, and the
most unlikely of relationships to develop.

A New Way

Here is what you can find in almost every bar during every
happy hour in America: mercy and grace on grand display.
You will find someone to speak with—often a stranger—
someone to listen, someone who might buy you a drink,
someone who will give you a ride.

Surely we can find the grace to accept and love one another within our church relationships, whether or not we are
seated within the same four walls each Sunday. Allow Jesus'

words in John 13:35 to resonate in your heart: *"By this all people will know that you are My disciples: if you have love for one another."*

Think of how silly it is for a Christian to believe God has much use for them in sharing His love with a lost and dying world when they cannot love one another. Resentment of others robs the worship of God so often. How can one expect to worship God for all He is with less than who we are? It just does not make sense.

The apostle John gives us a more intimate version of loving one another, where he records Jesus saying, *"I am giving you a new commandment, that you love one another; just as I have loved you, that you also love one another."* (John 13:34). Now, the commandment to love one another was not new. Deuteronomy 6:5 and Leviticus 19:18 commanded love for God and one another. But Jesus added something profound to this teaching. He was not only telling them to love—He set the example of ultimate love. He has truly left us with a template for forgiveness, love, and relationships. And to ensure our success, Christ has given the gift of His indwelling presence in each believer, which makes this love doable.

Read what Paul wrote to Titus regarding our relationship with other people: *"For we too **were once** foolish, disobedient, deceived, enslaved to various lusts and pleasures, spending our life in **malice and envy, hateful, hating one another,"** (Titus 3:3, emphasis mine). Paul's words remind us that these are the characteristics of the unsaved. This is how people treat themselves and each other before salvation.

However, do not be downtrodden, for Paul continues by saying, ***"But when** the kindness of God our Savior and His love for mankind appeared, He saved us, not on the basis of deeds which we did in righteousness, but in accordance with*

His mercy, by the washing of regeneration and renewing by the Holy Spirit," (Titus 3:4–5, emphasis mine).

So yes, there was a time when each of us handled life and relationships according to the rules of the flesh, for when we were prisoners to the flesh, we simply had no choice. "But when" your heart accepted Christ, scripture indicates that the old relationship model is to be done away with, and the Holy Spirit is to be what guides us. It just does not make any sense for a "verse four and five believer" to act like a "verse three non-believer."

Ah, but relationships can be hard; that's why we need Christ.

Follow the Recipe

I am an extrovert. I am often characterized as what people call a people person, in that I have always enjoyed being around others, can connect with just about anyone, will speak with anyone, and get energy from a crowd. I picked it up from my dad, as he also seemed to be able to connect or communicate with just about anyone. Additionally, I never remember my father ever speaking differently about or to any person because of their race, color, or socio-economic status. In fact, my dad seemed to always pull for the under-dog, which makes our crimes so much more puzzling. We certainly waged a war on the weak. Anyway, my sister and I grew up that way—always just enjoying all people.

I remember helping my mom once with her Texas Sheet Cake. Somewhere along the line, I made a crucial mistake; we never were quite sure what I slipped into the recipe, but the cake hit the trash can. I tried my best, but I was in a hurry, and though it seemed simple, I just could not duplicate the pro—my mom. We also fail in relationships when we fail to duplicate the pro—Jesus Christ. Remember Colossians 3:4, which says that Christ is our life. We fail in relationships when we attempt to *add* Christ instead of surrendering to Him.

Just like my cake recipe, I also had the wrong ingredients necessary for healthy and Godly relationships. It was not having relationships that was the problem, but rather how to create and enjoy a healthy relationship. I discovered I was putting too much weight on the other person in my relationships—not in the sense of my actual tangible demands from someone, but rather I believed that relationships with certain folks added value to my life and a lack of a relationship lessened my value.

But now, modeling my relationships after Christ, I have entered the Promised Land. I do not need to name drop or tear down someone else to feel better. I would rather spend my energy trying to help people spiral upwards than downwards. This especially applies to my brothers and sisters in Christ. I hope that as you rest in the Promised Land, enjoying the abundance, blessings, and forgiveness of Christ, that you will always remember there are others there as well. The land is best enjoyed in relationship.

Reflection Questions

1. What were your relationships like before your relationship with Christ? How do they compare to your relationships now?

2. Do you find yourself looking for meaning in relationships? Do you define your worth by who you surround yourself with?

IN PURSUIT OF THE PROMISED LAND

3. What relationships do you have that deepen your relationship with Christ? If you don't feel that you have any, how can you seek out people to join you on your faith journey?

4. How are you different from the people around you? How are you alike?

5. Do you tend to follow Pharisee relationship rules or Jesus' relationship rules?

6. Do you have a neighbor who you feel called to reach out to?

7. Do you need to pick up the phone or send an email today so you can reconcile or reconnect with someone?

10

WHERE THE PROMISED LAND IS FOUND

Where to Go from Here

So far we've spent this entire book looking at the dangers of different false Promised Lands—things that we pursue instead of God—and how they hurt us. The temptation of pursuing the wrong Promised Land will always exist until our Lord returns. Man's heart is selfish and shortcut-driven. God defined the problem in one verse: *"The heart is more deceitful*

than all else And is desperately sick; Who can understand it?" (Jeremiah 17:9).

But if the Promised Land is not found in pleasure, power, possessions, position, performance, or people ... then where *is* the Promised Land found? And how to we give up pie-in-the-sky for everlasting nourishment?

The First Heart

To answer this, we must look to our hearts. That is because we all have a sick heart. But which heart is sick? There are two hearts in every person.

First, let's talk about the one in the center of our chest. Often when hearing someone talk about heart health, the conversation includes a healthy diet, lifestyle, and exercise.

Several years ago, at the encouragement of my doctor, my wife, and my daughter, I began to implement the three aforementioned areas with sincerity. Each morning I leave the house to go walking, often with Judy in tow. Sometimes I flirt with a stress test on my knees by jogging. My doctor says walking is great, cardio is preferred when possible, and "Do not forget body squats," as walking alone does not build the leg strength needed as we grow older to get in and out of a seated position. But his focus is heart health. My exercise is often followed with some great nourishment provided by Judy's dynamite blends of protein, almond milk, blueberries, and a frozen banana.

And it is not only my doctor; scripture supports a healthy heart as well. As scriptures tells us, *"Or do you not know that your body is a temple of the Holy Spirit within you, whom you have from God, and you are not your own? For you have been bought for a price: therefore glorify God in your body."* (1 Corinthians 6:19–20). Paul says in verse 13, " ... **the body is** *not for sexual immorality, but **for the Lord, and the Lord is for the body,***" (emphasis mine). It honors Christ when we, to the best of our abilities, take care of our bodies.

Now, for the obvious, unwelcome news: one day our heart is going to give out. This fleshly heart is only going to take us so far, with an average life expectancy around 77–78 years. So far, we have a 100 percent mortality rate in this world, and unless the Lord tarries in His return, that number will go unchanged. The Apostle Paul knew that one day he would be leaving this earth, but he knew where he was going, as we learn in 2 Corinthians 5:8 where he said, *"but we are of good courage and prefer rather to be absent from the body and to be at home with the Lord."*

Paul knew one day his heart would stop, and he would leave this earth and would instantly be in the presence of Christ. So, bottom line, you can be on the cover of *Muscle and Fitness* or *Women's Fitness* magazines, but one day, the prince turns into a frog, the princess into an old maid, and life is soon over. We all know this should not be depressing or surprising.

So why does our loving God give us a temporary fleshly heart? Number one, it keeps roughly five quarts of our blood circulating through the body, bringing life to our body. But secondly and more importantly, it is temporary because we were not created to live on this earth for too long. We do not need a physical heart that could beat for eternity. That is because this is not our home; this body and earth are both temporary dwelling places.

Scripture gives many examples of the brevity of life here on earth. Here are just a few.

1 Chronicles 29:10–15 records a beautiful prayer of praise by King David. He was elated over the gathered assembly and the offering that had been given for the building of the Temple. In his prayer, he recognizes that everything stems

from and belongs to God. He also recognizes at best he is here for a moment: *"For we are strangers before You, and temporary residents, as all our fathers were; our days on the earth are like a shadow, and there is no hope."* (verse 15). David knew there was no hope for anything eternal here on this earth. He certainly had the ownership versus stewardship thing figured out. Everything belongs to God; we are leaving with zero in tow.

Secondly, how about Jesus' oldest half-brother, James? What did he say? *"Yet you do not know what your life will be like tomorrow. For you are just a vapor that appears for a little while, and then vanishes away."* (James 4:14). Light a match and watch the smoke quickly disappear.

Thirdly, Moses records a beautiful prayer in Psalm 90, where he states in verse 10, *"As for the days of our life, they contain seventy years, Or if due to strength, eighty years, Yet their pride is only trouble and tragedy; For it quickly passes, and we disappear."*

The scriptures are plentiful regarding this subject, but you get the point; life is short. So no, we were not created for the long haul physically. God does not want us on earth living in this physical body forever. Thank goodness, as I seem to be at the age where gravity is winning the battle. *But,* God does have eternity prepared for our hearts. There are numerous scriptures reflecting this truth. Enjoy this reassuring promise from King Solomon: *"He [God] has made everything appropriate in its time. He has also set eternity in their heart ... "* (Ecclesiastes 3:11a). Additionally, Solomon also spoke these words in Proverbs 23:26: *"Give me your heart, my son, And let your eyes delight in my ways."*

The Father, God, is pictured issuing an order to His son. "Give me your heart," God says. How about one of the better-known scriptures, found in 1 Samuel 16:7, where God is directing Samuel in finding the king that would rule Israel: *"But the Lord said to Samuel, 'Do not look at his appearance or at the height of his stature, because I have rejected him; for God does not see as man sees, since man looks at the outward appearance, but the Lord looks at the heart.'"* Truly, God is interested in your spiritual heart.

I remember reading these scriptures early in my Christian walk. Their message was a mystery to me. I had grown up and lived for much of my life focused on what impact my life could make here on earth. Certainly nothing flawed about that, as each of us wants to be remembered. But as my walk with Christ has matured, the memories I hope to leave behind have reorganized. I do hope and pray that my spouse, kids, family, and friends remember the good and funny times, and even the rough times, but with the flavor of perseverance. We all have memories. Our minds are recorders, documenting events into categories—name a subject and your mind searches for a file quickly producing a recollection of a time long gone by.

I hope I have left some good files behind; I feel confident I have. But here is where the change has happened: now, when I am gone, I hope and pray that not long after saying my name, that the name of Christ is soon mentioned. All sorts of other stuff may follow, but I hope the name of Christ comes out first. The very best thing I can leave behind for my family is an example of a heart that was set on eternity. My buddy Dwight Bain often reminds me that "inheritance is to leave things to someone, while legacy is to leave character to someone."

The Second Heart

In addition to the heart in our chests, we also have a second heart—the spiritual heart that we give to God. To the Greeks, the heart was the epicenter of man, the very seat of intellect, emotions, and our soul. The Greek word for heart, "kardia," is used over 800 times in the scriptures, all without ever referring to our physical blood pumping machine. It is this heart that drives passion in a person. It is this heart that connects with others. It is where love begins and ends.

Solomon certainly knew the expanse of the heart when he said, *"Watch over your heart with all diligence, For from it flow the springs of life."* (Proverbs 4:23). The wisest and wealthiest womanizer ever to live knew that everything flows from the heart. As we saw in 1 Samuel 16, the heart is where God does His examination of a person. This spiritual heart is where God communicates with His children. It is the spiritual heart, not the physical heart, that will see God, as stated in Matthew 5:8: *"Blessed are the pure in heart, for they will see God."*

Remember the old military recruitment posters where Uncle Sam said, "I want you"? Well, God is saying He wants you. He wants your heart—all of it, not part of it. God does not work in percentages or fractions. I tried that early on in my Christian walk, sometimes offering a decent percentage of myself to the Lord. The result? Well, I discovered that a heart set on 90 percent obedience eventually turns into a heart producing 100 percent disobedience. Proverbs 3:5 sums up well the percentage in which God operates: *"Trust in the Lord with all your heart And do not lean on your own understanding."*

Did you see the word "all"? You know what all means? It simply means *all.* It is like trying to sort-of shoot a gun— doesn't work. You either pull the trigger and *boom,* or you do not.

What is this giving *all* to God? It is the intentional giving of every fiber of your being—your very heart, soul, and strength over to the Lord and trusting in Him. Here is the beauty of giving our all: God does not allow you to out-give Him. I love the promise of Proverbs 3:6: *"In all your ways acknowledge Him, And He will make your paths straight."*

Len once explained this concept to me using a traffic policeman as his example. "Mike, you can ask that fellow over there for directions," he said as he pointed, "and I imagine he will tell you exactly what you need: second street on right, third street on your left, first street you come to, take a left and you will find your place. But God does not work like that. He does not point and send you off, He goes with you and guides you."

Now, you might be saying, "No one can be all-in, all the time." That is correct, but here is a story to help explain the all-in commitment.

Perhaps my favorite employee of all time was a lady who worked at one of our restaurants servicing the salad bar. The salad bar was large, with over fifty items, and the restaurant was busy. She was a delightful lady, but she had some challenges. She had some mental handicaps that at times would cause her to lose focus, or perhaps even seem to disconnect from people for a moment, perhaps leaving her position and going to sit in the break room. But she stands above everyone else who has ever worked for me for one reason. She showed up every day—and I mean every single shift—seeking to give 100 percent of her effort. She was so committed, so focused, so determined to do her job right that at times I thought her life depended on it. She was a joy to be around. Often her work ethic was contagious, and others would be inspired.

But here is the truth about her performance: oftentimes her efforts provided only about 75 percent of what we really needed. And when that happened, we just got her some help. I was never bothered, though, by the extra payroll dollars needed to support her, simply because of the way she showed up each day. On the contrary, I had employees who were operating without a handicap who showed up each day with the mindset of "I am giving about 75 percent effort today."

Here is the thing about an employee who comes in with a 75 percent attitude. In the end, their effort produces about a consistent 50 percent effort—and that did not cut it. Bottom line, if you aim for 100, you may get an average of 75 ... but if you aim for 75, the average is going to be 50 at best. And that will not produce the results needed.

I have found that in my Christian walk, it takes a daily made-up mind to serve Christ. My life with Christ is based on a trust that operates one day at a time. There is so much relief in knowing that I do not have to concern myself with being a follower of Christ, a good Christian husband, a good Christian father, or anything Christian, *tomorrow*. It is impossible to be something *tomorrow,* when it is still *today*. Yes, we plan our budgets, vacations, investments, and such, but this walk with Christ is for *today*. It is, as my buddy Eric states, "an intentional act."

My buddy in Orlando, Mr. Greg, tells me, "It just doesn't happen; we have to show up." In my life, when my heart has been set on less than 100 percent commitment to Christ, I always end up with a less-than day or season. Make up your mind to serve Christ today—write that on a piece of paper, place it in your car, on your desk, or on one of your five index cards.

Christ's Love—The Fee

As my life has matured in Christ, I have learned to never lose sight of the cross. My early years were spent in celebration as I moved away from the cross—not moving away as in sin, but rather, a moving away from that remembrance of Christ hanging on the cross. It had become too easy and convenient to lose sight of the cross, too easy to lose sight of the death that I had bypassed, too easy to speak of the cross as if it was the entrance unto eternal life without remembering the sacrifice of my Savior. Yes, I know that sin requires a payment, and that payment is death. The only access to God is through that payment. Additionally, there is only one man who can make that payment. I, of course, know that it is Christ who made and makes that payment. He is pleased to make that payment for all who seek and ask. But, after that initial transaction, at times I have been guilty of forgetting. Let me explain what helps me remember.

As I write this, Easter is fast approaching. One of the television channels has been promoting the movie *The Passion of the Christ*. Perhaps you saw that movie. Here is what I think upon when just hearing the title, without even seeing the movie again.

The movie had a run time of 127 minutes, of which about 100 minutes of it was centered around the torture, whipping, scourging, and crucifixion of Christ. When I first saw the movie, I wept bitterly as I watched Christ suffer and die. The actor, Jim Caviezel, was amazing in his performance. But here is my reflection regarding the movie: as brutal as that movie portrayed the crucifixion of our Lord and all the events leading up to it, the movie only lasted 127 minutes. This pales in comparison to the actual length of time in which Jesus was tortured and crucified. (Yes, I know, no one would go see a 15-hour movie but hang in there with me.)

Here is a quick timeline. Jesus is arrested sometime the night before Good Friday, perhaps near midnight. Judas betrays Christ with a kiss. Jesus is taken before Annas, then Caiaphas, where the Sanhedrin would be waiting for Him.

False witnesses give their testimony. He is mocked, slapped, and his clothes are torn. The torture of Christ has started. By 6 a.m. Jesus appears before Pilate, is then sent to Herod, then is sent back to Pilate. He is beaten and scourged, then he is sentenced to be crucified. Mark 15:25 tells us, *"Now it was the third hour when they crucified Him,"* which is 9 a.m. Finally, at the ninth hour, 3 p.m., Christ dies. This entire process from arrest to death takes about 15 hours.

On top of that, my heart reminds me many times of Isaiah 53, in which 700 years before Christ's death, the prophet Isaiah gives a description of our Lord's death on the cross. Then my heart leaps to Isaiah 52:14, which states, *"Just as many were appalled at you,* My people, *So His appearance was marred beyond* that of a *man, And His form beyond the sons of mankind."*

Isaiah refers to this person as a servant in verse 13. The meaning of verse 14 is astonishing, as it reveals that the servant of verse 13 would be so brutally beaten and tortured that He would no longer be recognizable as a human. Now, with that verse on my lips, the pictures in my mind take me back to the closing of the movie. I could still tell that was Jim Caviezel on the cross.

These are my first thoughts about Easter—not the movie, but Christ on the cross. Yes, I know the tomb is empty and sin, death, and the grave have been defeated, but before that, Christ took that punishment for me. Additionally, I always think of Matthew 26:53, where Jesus is speaking to His captors, under arrest, facing a sham trial, knowing what was coming: *"Or do you think that I cannot appeal to My Father, and He will at once put at My disposal more than twelve legions of angels?"*

What? He could have prayed and stopped the whole thing. This is so contrary to the world's thinking. Of course, His lack of speaking produced the best unprayed prayer. Think about it—if Jesus had called on those 12 legions of angels, His torture and crucifixion would have been halted immediately. There would be no cross, no burial, no resurrection, and no victory over sin and death. Mankind would be destined to die in their sins with no hope of redemption.

I contrast that picture of Christ on the cross with the stack of stuff for which I have been forgiven—the things my mouth has uttered or the perverse things my heart has shouted. I can only fall to my knees and thank our Lord. I deserved death, but Christ went to the cross so that I might live. I am afraid that at times, without a made-up mind and an intentional spirit, I am too good at forgetting instead of remembering. So my prayer time each morning begins with a moment of reflection on Christ's sacrifice for me. I then move on and celebrate the whole package: His crucifixion, death, burial, and resurrection. It is this work of Christ that made a way for me to enter the Promised Land.

Heart Versus Head—The Entrance

We have been created for eternity. Our heart is spiritual, and God desires access to our hearts. Many of you have already experienced that life-changing moment of inviting Christ into your life, but perhaps some of you are still focused on your physical heart alone. I hope and pray you have read the scriptures throughout this book, but for now, let us focus on one:

" ... that if you confess with your mouth Jesus as Lord, and believe in your heart that God raised Him from the dead, you will be saved," (Romans 10:9).

Remember the definition of heart—the spiritual heart. That is where belief resides. No, it is not a simpleton's belief where the mind is dismissed, but the heart is the center of your life. For years, the eighteen inches from my brain to my heart separated me from the love, forgiveness, and grace of Christ. I knew *of* Christ; I knew Jesus died on a cross in the same way I knew George Washington was the first president. I knew information regarding Christ and our first President all as head knowledge. Plain and simple, I knew lots of facts. There was no heart involved. On that September day in 1997, I transferred my desire to know Christ from solely head knowledge to a heart confirmation. Remember how I said "I know something has happened," right after I invited Christ into my heart? I did not understand intellectually, and yes, I have had thousands of questions along the way, but I have asked them all from within the relationship with Christ. I went ahead and jumped all in with my heart, and slowly my brain caught up.

I speak weekly with folks regarding questions about Christ, the Bible, and my beliefs. There are such good questions, as so many folks are deep thinkers. I myself, ask questions each time I study and prepare for a lesson. But I am always seeking to draw closer to Christ, not put distance between Him and me. As I have engaged more people in discussion over the years, there has been a clear definable difference between questions that are seeking truth and those that are seeking to tear down. I spend my time where truth is being sought. Time is short and arguing someone to Christ has never proven successful. When dealing with difficult questions, I also am not afraid to give this answer: "I do not know that answer, but I will do my best to find out and get back with you."

But please listen: if it is questions that you need answered, if it is the mind you are trying to appease, or if your effort to know Christ is only related to your brain, then Satan will make sure to have enough questions to carry you to your last breath. Perhaps it is time to pause and reflect on the words of Romans 10:9. Is God calling you to Himself? Go and read the "Romans Road" scriptures. Do you sense a voice moving from your head to your heart? God is speaking to your heart. Or, perhaps, do you need to rededicate your life to Christ? Seize this moment and open your heart to Christ. Stop right now and get on your knees, sit in your chair, get on the floor—do whatever it takes. Cry out to God and ask Him to take you into His Promised Land.

Rejoice in this promise: *"By this the love of God was revealed in us, that God has sent His only Son into the world so that we may live through Him."* (1 John 4:9). There is life and infinite fullness in Christ. If you have made that decision, call a Christian friend, call a pastor, but please share. God's people want to celebrate with you.

Closing Thoughts

Our heart is wicked because it does not desire God or the things of God. As you have read, my heart sought to ruthlessly position myself ahead of God. The "I want it now" passion and pursuit continually robs everyone of God's provisions. This is understandable to those outside of a relationship with Christ, but what is disheartening is the P.I.G. (Problem with Immediate Gratification) disease that is rampant even amongst believers. Believers can get stuck, I know—I have needed the tow truck on many occasions. Often my temptation to hold onto what is present exceeds any desire to exercise the faith needed to obtain a greater possession. Thus, in the end, I have settled for a land just short of the Promised Land.

I have learned that Satan's craftiness makes for provisions in this land. He will allow you to become settled and grounded in the land of infinite finiteness. One may find peace, prosperity, and pleasure, but only as the world is able to provide. I have been back to that land of illusion.

Where are you? Perhaps you are a believer in Christ, living one day at a time surrendered to Him as Lord of your life. You know that your life is His life. Or possibly you are a believer who still struggles to believe the promises of God and rest in His Promised Land. You have been delivered from the enslavement to sin, but you have not yet entered His rest. You may rejoice over the deliverance from the "wages of sin" (Romans 6:23), but you are ignorant to the fact that God is focused on more than just a deliverance. Or perhaps you are not sure of your relationship with God. Well, this Old Testament story paints a picture for each group.

This story is found in Numbers 32. This chapter gives us some interesting information regarding the tribes of Gad, Reuben, and half the tribe of Manasseh. But first, a little background. Forty years of wilderness wandering had come to an end, and the new generation of God's children were about to enter the Land God had prepared. Forty years of anticipation and dreaming were about to become a reality. They were battle-tested, as they had defeated the armies of Amalek, Arad, the Amorites, Bashan, and the Midianites. God had protected His children. Often the victor in battle enjoyed the spoils of his conquest, so the victory had provided gold, jewelry, and such, but also provided an abundance of livestock. Sheep and cattle were captured in large numbers. The spoils of war had been divided amongst the tribes—all the tribes, including those who fought and those who stayed behind. God's grace was equally distributed.

So with the memory of the past forty years confirming the Lord's protection, favor, and victory, Joshua was set to lead the people across the Jordan River and into the Promised Land. They were poised to receive what God had promised forty years earlier. As the armies sat near the eastern bank of the Jordan River—in a land once inhabited by their enemies, but at that point mostly filled with livestock—the leaders of Gad and Reuben made an astonishing request. It is recorded in Numbers 32:5, *"And they said, 'If we have found favor in your sight, let this land be given to your servants as our property; do not take us across the Jordan.'"*

This is another one of those head-scratching moments for me. If I was in Joshua's shoes, I would have said "Okay, let me get this straight. For forty years we wandered through the wilderness. We watched our parents and grandparents die in the wilderness. We ate manna for forty years. We have been talking about this day 24/7 for forty years, and now you want to stay just outside the Promised Land?"

There are some commentators who suggest this story reflects God's grace and provisions for His children and an extension of His promise to all the lands, both east and west of the Jordan River. Also, God clearly allows them to settle on the west side. I will leave that debate to the theologians. But I believe along with many commentators that this portrays a perfect picture of settling for less than the best.

In verse 5, the people of Gad say, "if we have found grace in **your** sight," (emphasis mine). Problem number one: they are looking for favor from Moses instead of God. I can tell you; I have missed out on plenty as I sought the favor of man and not God—and so have you. God is the decision-maker on your Promised Land, not a man. Moses' first response is spot on. Verses 6b–7 record, *"'Should your brothers go to war while you remain here? And why are you discouraging the sons of Israel from crossing over into the land which the Lord has given them?'"* Moses was telling them that a fearful attitude can be contagious.

As I reflect on my walk, too often I have allowed the lack of faith in others to infiltrate my faith like cancer, slowly spreading disease and doubt. Additionally, I have allowed my discontent and fear to impact others. Moses knew discouragement came not only with a voice, but also with actions. Even if there was no cry against going forward, their action of not pressing forward spoke louder than any words. It is easy, especially in the church, to find "me too" friends—friends who have the same opinion as you when it comes to complaining. Bottom line, if you complain to enough people, eventually someone will say "Yeah, me too." Then the two of you together will be miserable. God's people need to surround themselves with "going people" who walk in faith. God is looking for a "going people" who are waiting on a "coming Lord."

When God is calling you to enter His Land, stay away from the naysayers. Think about it; how can what we possess be better than what God wants to provide? Sure, the west side of the Jordan River was great cattle country. But I must believe that the sovereignty of God, forty years earlier, knew all that was needed in His provisions for His people. In the end, it came down to the promise of God vs. the promise of cattle. Eventually, an arrangement was crafted: Gad and Reuben would go across the river and help subdue the land, defeat the enemies, and when the land was at peace, they would return to the west side of the river. Seems like a distant second-place finish.

Every year, I love watching all the championship events. I may not watch much baseball or basketball during the season, but I watch the championship games. I love that championship moment when years of hard work pay off with winning the title, especially in college sports where so much real passion is displayed. In all my years of watching championship events, I have never seen the champion team win and then walk off the field with no celebration. I have never seen them leave the trophy on the field. Nope; they want that trophy. It is a reminder of the perseverance and discipline of the previous years. Joshua and the two million Jews were champions. God had provided the victories. But Gad and Reuben were intentionally walking away from God's trophy, His Promised Land.

Please remember this: the same faith that had brought them out of Egypt was the same faith needed to enter God's Promised Land.

There was no need for a double shot of faith, no extra dose required to enter the Promised Land. It was simply faith—belief and trust. The same faith Israel had practiced some forty years earlier in walking out of slavery is the exact faith they needed to enter the Land. Too often in my life I have exercised great faith in my own faith; a poor choice, as my faith wobbles at best. Rather it is where I have placed my faith—in our Lord and Savior Jesus Christ—that makes the difference. Faith exercised without Christ is simply wishing on a star: lots of light, but no life.

There are two more verses for review which are important for your heart's fulfillment. In Numbers 32:11, Moses reminds Gad of the previous forty years and the judgment of God upon Israel for their failure to walk by faith into the Promised Land, saying, *"'None of the men who came up from Egypt, from twenty years old and upward, shall see the land which I swore to Abraham, to Isaac, and to Jacob; for they did not follow Me fully.'"* Moses was telling Gad, "If you are not fully committed, you too will fall away." He confirms that in verse 12: *"'except Caleb the son of Jephunneh the Kenizzite and Joshua the son of Nun; for they have followed the Lord fully.'"*

In my experience, I have found that commitment is mandatory. Though God is surely able, He does not drag His children kicking and screaming into His rest. There is no free ticket, no free ride into the Promised Land. It comes from a heart that has surrendered fully unto the Lord and desires to walk in obedience. Remember, this is not an obedience to keep you in your eternal security, but rather to *"keep yourselves in the love of God,"* (Jude 1:21a). It's the desire to stay in the place where God can work in your life. Here is the beautiful, mind-blowing part about a full-heart commitment to the Lord that takes you to His Promised Land—the battle and the provisions will always belong to God. I finally discovered, just as the Jewish children did, that it has not been my participation in the battles that was so crucial, but rather my faith and commitment to Christ. You can never fight hard enough to win a battle that has already been won.

So what happened to Gad and Reuben? Eventually, these tribes would be carried away by the Assyrians, and they would be no more. As I reflect, I cannot help but think of the example my early life had demonstrated to my children. They were so close to seeing their dad settle for the Promised Land of man's provisions. Even as a believer, at times I have settled for the shortcut, stopped briefly in the wrong land, or pursued something outside of God's plan.

It's Time to Make a Change

Far too many Christians have halted from walking into the Promised Land. No wonder the church is less impactful in our world, especially here in America. We have settled for less and become complacent, in line with and accepting the world's standard. I had a young man tell me at the union mission some time ago, "It seems to me the church is no different than what is on the streets." Ouch, that hurts.

Perhaps it is because there are too many desert wanderers. These wanderers are represented by the children that walked in the desert for forty years; worldly at times, close to faith at times. Sometimes they were near the Promised Land, but at other times they were near Egypt—a pinball group of people. If you remember, their failure of faith to move forward into the Promised Land early on resulted in the judgment of God. Those who were twenty years or older would not enter the Promised Land. For forty years they walked, having just enough of God to leave Egypt, but still too much Egypt to enter the Promised Land.

God does not desire wilderness wanderers. This makes a mockery of God's deliverance from Egypt. When we as followers of Christ wander in the wilderness, we make a mockery of grace. Be a person who remembers. Remember the cross, for there is no such thing as cheap grace. How could there be? Christ died on the cross so that we might receive grace. Think on our Lord's words: *"But Jesus said to him, 'No man, after putting his hand to the plow and looking back, is fit for the kingdom of God.'"* (Luke 9:62). God does not want admirers of the old life and the old land. Set your face toward the Promised Land.

I hope and pray you will enter the fullness of the Promised Land and stay there. Do not settle for vacations or long weekends. More than likely, you have researched extensive lands only to find limited fulfillment, eventually finding emptiness. There is a rest that is unparalleled in the Promised Land of our Lord. Think about what the apostle Paul writes: *"For as many as the promises of God are, in Him they are yes; therefore through Him also is our Amen to the glory of God through us."* (2 Corinthians 1:20). Paul spells it out. All the Old Testament promises, all the New Testament promises, the promises of peace and provision, the promise of present and future salvation—all of this is wonderfully found in Jesus Christ.

Do the Work

But the Promised Land is not the lazy man's land, though the writer of Hebrews states beautifully, *"Consequently, there remains a Sabbath rest for the people of God. For the one who has entered His rest has himself also rested from his works, as God did from His."* (Hebrews 4:9–10). Yes, there is rest, and I have found it. But there is clearly something that this passage says and something that it does not say. First, it says that the rest belongs to Christ. Second, it does *not* say that we sit on our laurels and don't participate.

While in prison, I wrote these words in my Bible: "Without Christ I can't, but without me, He won't; therefore, no laziness." Let me explain. I have spoken with plenty of men who say they are trusting in God to land a job, but they do not knock on doors and fill out applications; plenty of folks who want God to heal their marriage, but there is no unity in obedience to the scriptures; and plenty of guys with addictions, but they do not heed a single verse regarding temptation.

Our walk in Christ demands effort.

I have learned that my Christian life should not be related to only a simple date on the calendar. Though that is the day that my heart and life was spiritually changed forever, and I entered the spiritual Promised Land, it has been a daily life of drawing closer to God through prayer, obedience, repentance, and service that has kept me feasting in the land of fulfillment. There is no wall keeping me in the Land; I have been able to leave and seek elsewhere. God has allowed that freedom. But when I have moved outside our Lord's boundaries, the results have been ugly. So it has been a daily practice to surrender and walk.

Each day I have learned that I must put my feet to my faith, and my friend, so should you. The Christian life must be in the pursuit of obedience to experience God's full abundance. Not perfection—I have been far from perfect (but you already know that). That is why we have the promise of 1 John 1:9: *"If we confess our sins, He is faithful and righteous, so that He will forgive us our sins and cleanse us from all unrighteousness."*

I will remind you again that this is not an obedience to keep your position in Christ. You are seated in heavenly places; you are in Christ, and Christ is in you. There is nothing that is going to change that. God has no erasers for the names that are written in the book of life. But remember and practice Jude's words in Jude 1:21: *"keep yourselves in the love of God, looking forward to the mercy of our Lord Jesus Christ to eternal life."* What is he saying? He is saying to keep yourself in the place, the Promised Land, where God can bless you.

Stay put! God is not in the business of blessing His children when they are not where they are supposed to be, doing what they are not supposed to be doing. There is a new strain of Christianity today that seems to speak of the abundance of God's love without referencing His holiness. There is not a wall of love that protects us from His holiness. On the contrary, God's love radiates because of His holiness. God is holy; stay holy in your commitment to Him.

I hope and pray that God's commitment to you, demonstrated by the crucifixion of His Son, will move your heart as God calls you to settle in His Promised Land. As Jude said, *" ... looking forward to the mercy of our Lord Jesus Christ to eternal life."* (verse 21). In other words, live as if Christ is coming back *today.*

Years ago my mentor Len made this observation: "Mike, I have been a Christian for nearly thirty years and have never met a man yet that said giving his life to Christ was a poor decision." Len is now 89 years old. I saw him recently; it has now been 61 years, and as he says he still hasn't met that person. Len was correct—I have never felt alone, and I have always known my Lord's presence. With Christ, on a day-to-day commitment I have been able to give up "pie" and find fulfillment in the Promised Land.

Reflection Questions

1. Does your spiritual heart get the same workout as your physical heart?

2. What is keeping you from surrendering your heart to the Lord? Be honest and open and share your struggles and thoughts. What do you have to lose?

3. Does your life reflect a view of eternity or of the present?

4. Do you struggle with the word "all"? If so, why? Do you ever attempt to work off percentages? What percentage are you bringing to the table each day?

5. Are you wandering in the wilderness? What keeps you in the wilderness and out of the Promised Land?

6. Is your walk resting only in grace and ignoring obedience? What steps can you take to increase your obedience?

7. Which pie are you getting rid of today? How can you get help to stay off the "pie diet?" Who can you partner with as an accountability partner?

8. Are you ready to rewrite your life-redefining sentence? Are you willing to write your sentence and share it with your spouse, kids, and friends?

9. How has your life-defining sentence changed? What help will you need to stay committed to the changes you made?

11

CONCLUSION

The Coffin

I mentioned earlier in the book that Judy has a phrase for me when my attitude gets out of line. "You need to get back in your coffin!" she tells me firmly. I would like to say that months go by without me hearing that phrase, or even better, without even getting *that look* which says the phrase just as well. But that is not so. The pattern usually follows this

routine: I am in my feelings about something, Christ is not being glorified by my actions or words, Judy issues the reminder, and off I go to my upstairs sanctuary, which is my office. This is where I work at getting back into the coffin.

The phrase "Get back in your coffin," is a play on the words of Romans 6, where Paul refers to a believer's death in Christ. Paul makes it clear that a Christian is no longer a prisoner to sin, as he explains that a believer is dead unto the power of sin. Simply put, the old guy that lived before he met Christ is now dead. Yet, somehow, that dead guy rears his ugly head from time to time—hence Judy's statement. Upon hearing those words, I know (and she knows) that I am soon to be office-bound. It may take a moment for my heart to follow, but my feet move up the stairs to my office chair. Upon arrival, my thoughts are the same each time. Why does that dead man still seek to come back to life? What wakes him up? Those questions have been answered for me by walking through the promises and truths of scripture.

How to Put the Dead Man Back

Here is the culmination of the truths I have learned while sitting in my office chair: when Christ redeemed my soul at salvation, He did not redeem my flesh. Our earthly flesh is certainly not redeemed this side of heaven (1 Corinthians 15:35-58) nor will our flesh nature ever make peace with our new life in Christ. Nope, the natural man remains natural. This thought was a struggle for me as a new believer. The idea that I could sin again seemed contrary to what a "new" Mike should look and act like. How could a Christian still struggle with some of the same temptations? At times my mind wanted to refute my salvation and eternal security. Yet, my heart told me I was different.

The following verse has been an anchor to my soul: *"Therefore if anyone is in Christ, this person is a new creation; the old things passed away; behold, new things have come."* (2 Corinthians 5:17). You want to talk about forgiveness and grace? Let that verse sink in. Yet as I mentioned above, my mind would ask questions: *If I am a new creature, why do the old habits still pop up?* and even worse, *Am I really saved? Surely I should be acting better,* I often thought.

Then one day a light bulb went off as I was reading through the book of Romans—specifically Romans 6-8. The truths began to leap off the pages into my heart. I discovered that scripture never states that Christ came to make mankind better; never is it stated that the natural man will become an improved natural man. A re-reading of 5:17 proves this point, as there is nothing in that verse about improving, maturing, or getting better. Quite the opposite is stated, as it says a believer becomes a new person. There is no mention of improving on the old. It appears that the old guy is gone, passed away ... as in *dead.* What a blessing and relief to my heart and soul, as my heart held many secrets from the drug years.

So step #1 to putting the old man back in the coffin is recognizing that I am, and you are, a new creation in Christ. What a beautiful promise. Right at salvation we become new. We are given a new heart—not a changed heart, nor improved heart, but rather a transaction takes place where Christ exchanges His heart for our dead heart.

Step #2 to "getting back in the coffin" has been accepting that struggles and battles will continue as long as I am on this earth. Every believer should know this truth. If you have not wrestled with this, maybe it is time to search your heart and soul about your relationship with Christ. I have discovered that the enemy has been relentless. Each follower of

Christ knows all too well that there is a still a battle in our inner man. The enemy, inside of me, has been a formidable foe.

Paul brilliantly defines this battle against this flesh enemy in Romans chapter 7:14–25. Any cursory reading of this scripture is sure to leave a believer despondent, as he seems to portray a bleak picture of the Christian man. But I encourage you to read, study, meditate, and pray over these verses, as this passage is more than it seems.

Here is part of the grim picture: as he discusses his Christian life, Paul states in verse 18, *"For I know that good does not dwell in me, that is, in my flesh; for the willing is present in me, but the doing of the good is not."*

When I first read that, I thought, *Wow, I relate to that at times.* My inner man seemed to still have a production line which continued to produce sin.

What does one do with that verse?

Well, in my earlier years, I found some relief and excuses in that verse. How can you blame me for struggling if even the great apostle of the New Testament struggled? But although I knew I had to take sole ownership of that verse, my heart told me it was only half the truth for a believer. First, if good does not dwell in us, what is it that exists in me and each believer? It is the sin nature that relentlessly seeks to disclose itself through our mind and actions. It is when that nature is acted upon that the believer moves from having died in Christ to living again controlled by the flesh. The dead man arises from his coffin, as the flesh longs to live again in each follower of Christ.

This is where Satan does his best work. The church is filled with desert wanderers who have fallen victim to the revitalization of the flesh. It is not Satan who stands in our church parking lots shooing people away; it is the born-again believer who is living a flesh-controlled life. Their sins may be hidden, but quietly they remain flesh-controlled while calling themselves Christian. Remember, the flesh hates death. Thus the answer to why the flesh comes back to life. Why does the dead man arise? Simple—there is nothing a dead man craves more than to be alive again.

But do not despair, as Paul does not leave us helpless. He does not leave us to fight the old man to the point of exhaustion leading to failure. Help is on the way; but first, let's discover the root cause of what awakens the flesh.

So what wakes him up? Well, the flesh is at best a light sleeper. I have learned that the flesh is close—so close at times that you can feel his breath on your neck. Let me tell you what gets him out of his casket. I have found that each time I take that shortcut, each time I place myself ahead of Christ, each time I "do me" instead of allowing Christ to be the driving influence, I wake him up. It is amazing the flesh's ability to slip through even the slightest crack in any open door. If Christ is not preeminent in my life each day, then the old guy is apt to wake up. And when he gets through the door, most people resort to the flesh to fight.

The victory over the flesh never comes from a strong flesh. Jesus said, *"'If a house is divided against itself, that house will not be able to stand.'"* (Mark 3:25). I have attempted to fight the flesh with the flesh. Let me tell you this: *it never works.* So often it has ended in pain with much collateral damage.

Paul proves this point with his words in Romans 7:14: *"For we know that the Law is spiritual, but I am fleshly, sold into bondage to sin."* He is saying that there is no spiritual law that can help the flesh. I have tried. I have sat in my office, determined to be right, determined to stay stuck in the wrong attitude, at times purposely refusing to submit to God's nudging in my heart, using the time to devise a well laid-out fleshly response to deal with whatever issue sent me to my office initially ... all to no avail. Further, my observations usually reveal this truth that may be true for you as well—my unchecked thoughts, emotions, and misplaced expectations usually were the key to unlocking the coffin. And what do I mean by unchecked thoughts? Simple: Christ was left out and/or ignored. I have discovered that the flesh simply will not listen to the spirit. God will *never* make peace with your flesh.

The War Room

The battle is on. It is not a question of *when* you will battle so much as *how* you battle. So how have you battled the flesh? Are you prepared, or has your response been like mine at times? When my conscience is going in one direction and my actions are headed to another, I should stop. But a lot of times, I blow right past the Holy Spirit's stop sign and put the pedal to the floor. The flesh is always moving us forward toward destruction.

When I face these struggles, I tend to hesitate in my response spiritually, as I seek to push back the flesh—with my flesh. The result? Things escalate. A spark becomes a flame, and soon the "old man" is strutting his ego, pride, and self-sufficiency. Truly, a little leaven creates problems. The spiritual man has now given way to the dead man. "Back to your coffin," I tell my flesh, as my mind reflects on the admonishment from Judy. But the flesh resists. It *hates* to surrender. So when I first enter my office, it usually begins with me planting my flag of self-righteousness. But often something powerful happens when one places himself in the right place.

Off the bat, I will say this—there is nothing magical about

my office. But it is a place of spiritual warfare. It is in this room where many of my spiritual battles are fought. It is where I pray, where I read the scriptures, where I cry, where I meditate, where I write, where I intercede, and where I study. It is here where I am reminded often of what I have learned as I have grown in Christ. It is my place of close encounters with Christ. Is it the only place? No. Would you have the same experience in my office? I doubt it. But it has become a sanctuary for me.

Judy created this space for me six years ago. The walls are covered with stuff I like and things that have special meaning to me. The shelves are filled with a few hundred books pertaining to theology. The first thing hung on my wall is a note from Judy, which says "My prayer is that beautiful conversations are shared with you and God's Holy Spirit, as we offer our home, this room, and our individual hearts for His service."

Do you have a place to run to in your home? A place where calmness can prevail, and cotton can be moved from the ears to the mouth? If not, find that place. Create that place.

It is in this room where I face the battles Paul tells us about in the book of Romans. I love Romans 7:22, where Paul says *"For I joyfully agree with the law of God in the inner person."* Paul recognized that there was a new law—a different law— at work in his heart that agreed with God in His hatred of sin. We are not just left with words, but we are given the presence of Christ as our inner law. Paul knew that, as a new man in Christ, that there was a spiritual inner man pushing back against the flesh. His inner man now sought to take sides with the law of God, which is Christ.

Whenever I slow down and put the coffin escapee in my office chair, I am quickly aware of another voice in my heart. There is a divine voice pushing back against the dead man.

Paul seems to reverse course as he cries out *"Wretched man that I am! Who will set me free from the body of this death?"* (Romans 7:24). But the cavalry arrives, as if it is Christ riding his "white horse" (as seen in Revelation 19:11), when Paul states, *"Thanks be to God through Jesus Christ our Lord!"* (Romans 7:25).

Who delivers? Who puts the old guy back in the coffin? It is Christ Jesus our Lord. It is the promise of Christ *in us* and *us in Him* that provides deliverance. What unmitigated peace comes from that truth. Slowly, as I remind myself of Christ's eternal indwelling presence, the spirit man regains his life.

Here is one of my favorite glorious truths from scripture, found in Ephesians 2:4–5: *"But God, being rich in mercy, because of His great love with which He loved us, even when we were dead in our wrongdoings, **made us alive together with Christ** (by grace you have been saved),"* (emphasis mine). Finally the dead man is back in his casket. The same applies to you as a follower of Christ. Christ lives in you.

Jesus is about two types of deliverance: a deliverance *from* and a deliverance *into.* We are delivered *from* Egypt, delivered *from* the coffin. We are delivered *to* the Promised Land—His eternal fulfillment.

Moving Forward

I want to share with you two verses that the Holy Spirit uses to grab my attention. This is the part where the feet are applied to the faith—where effort is demanded. They coincide perfectly with the words I shared earlier from my buddies Eric and Mr. Greg.

The first is found in Galatians 5:16, where it says, *"But I say, walk by the Spirit, and you will not carry out the desire of the flesh."* Each day I have a choice: either the intentional decision to follow Christ, or the deliberate choice not to follow Him.

The second verse is found in Colossians 3:10: *"and have **put on** the new self, which is being renewed to a true knowledge according to the image of the One who created it ... "* (emphasis mine). Did you catch that? The verse says "put on." In other words, each day we are to "put on the new self," which tells me the old self did not just fall off. I have found that the "old guy" stays in the coffin when I intentionally and purposely put on the new self.

So who are you following? What are you putting on? I will answer for you and me: No greater than the person of Jesus Christ.

Maybe you're already saved, and you're saying to yourself, *Well, I already have Christ.* But how about appropriating what is available? When I intentionally stay connected to Christ, the coffin stays shut. So clothe yourself in Christ. Stay connected. Be intentional. Start today with your heart and mind made up to serve Christ. Stay in your coffin and enjoy the Promised Land.

Reflection Questions

1. In what situations do you find that you most need to "get back in the coffin"?

2. Do you have a "war room," or someplace where you can retreat when you need to "get back in the coffin"?

3. What differences do you see between your "dead man" and your "new man"?

4. What struggles and battles are you still fighting, despite being a new man?

5. Remember the "life-defining statement" that you wrote earlier in the book? How does your life-defining statement look different now than it did before?

6. What does the Promised Land look like for you?

ENDNOTES

1   Augustine of Hippo, Confessions, trans. Garry Wills (London, Penguin Classics, 2008).

2   "Pie in the Sky," Merriam-Webster Inc., Merriam-Webster's Dictionary of English Usage, Reprint Ed. (Springfield, Merriam-Webster Inc., 1994). https://www.merriam-webster.com/dictionary/pie%20in%20the%20sky.

3   "Passion", Merriam-Webster Inc., Merriam-Webster's Dictionary of English Usage, Reprint Ed. (Springfield, Merriam-Webster Inc., 1994.) https://www.merriam-webster.com/dictionary/passion.

4   Sager, M. (2015) Jack Nicholson's what I've learned: "my motto is: More good ... - esquire, Esquire. Accessed October 2nd, 2023. https://www.esquire.com/uk/culture/film/a4036/jack-nicholson-what-ive-learned/.

5   Rick Warren, Life: What on Earth Am I Here For? P. 17. (Grand Rapids, Zondervan, 2002).

6 William Blake, The Book of Thel. (N.p., DigiCat, 2022). Kindle.

7 Yogi Berra, 65 Motivational Yogi Berra Quotes For Success In Life. Overall Motivation, n.d. Accessed, October 2nd, 2023. https://www.overallmotivation.com/quotes/yogi-berra-quotes-life/.

8 "Definition of PLEASURE." Merriam-Webster: America's Most Trusted Dictionary. Last modified November 19, 2023. https://www.merriam-webster.com/dictionary/pleasure.

9 William Shakespeare, The Merry Wives of Windsor (New York City, Simon and Schuster, 2020).

10 Stu Weber, Spirit Warriors: A Soldier Looks at Spiritual Warfare. P. 150. (Colorado Springs, Multnomah, 2001).

11 "Power," Merriam-Webster Inc., Merriam-Webster's Dictionary of English Usage, Reprint Ed. (Springfield, Merriam-Webster Inc., 1994.) https://www.merriam-webster.com/dictionary/power.

12 Emily Schmall, "The Cult of Chick-Fil-A," Forbes July 6, 2007, https://www.forbes.com/forbes/2007/0723/080.html?sh=116805d75971.

13 Emily Schmall, "The Cult of Chick-Fil-A," Forbes July 6, 2007, https://www.forbes.com/forbes/2007/0723/080.html?sh=116805d75971.

14 "Performance," Merriam-Webster Inc., Merriam Webster's Dictionary of English Usage, Reprint Ed. (Springfield, Merriam-Webster Inc., 1994). https://www.merriam-webster.com/dictionary/performance.

15   Lou Holtz Quotes. BrainyQuote.com, BrainyMedia Inc, 2023. https://www.brainyquote.com/quotes/lou_holtz_383816, accessed October 24, 2023.

16   John MacArthur Jr., The MacArthur Study Bible, (Nashville, W Publishing Group, 1997).

17   Fred Boone, "Why Small Groups", Dynamic Small Groups, (website), accessed October 16, 2023, https://dynamicsmallgroups.org/.

ABOUT THE AUTHOR

 Mike Hardy's life plays out like a dramatic movie, with all of the ups and downs, twists and turns, as well as heartbreak and heart restoration. His life is a story of redemption. That's why he decided to write *In Pursuit of the Promised Land.* Driven with a desire to share how God changed a pleasure-seeking cocaine smuggler into a follower of Jesus Christ, Hardy embarked on this path to publication, paving it in much prayer and expectation of how God might use his story to help others find true peace. Hardy, who has a bachelor's degree in education and a master's degree in religious education, has spent over a decade teaching adult life groups and Sunday School classes, as well as serving as a volunteer preacher at Orlando Rescue Union Mission. Married for 10 years to his best friend, Judy, the Hardys make their home in the Sunshine State where they continue to follow God's calling for their lives.